Anti-Semitism and the Boycott, Divestment, and Sanctions Movement

Other Books in the Global Viewpoints Series

GLOBALVIEWPOINTS

Anti-Semitism and the Boycott, Divestment, and Sanctions Movement

Gary Wiener, Book Editor

GREENHAVEN
PUBLISHING

Published in 2019 by Greenhaven Publishing, LLC
353 3rd Avenue, Suite 255, New York, NY 10010

Copyright © 2019 by Greenhaven Publishing, LLC

First Edition

Articles in Greenhaven Publishing anthologies are often edited for length to meet page requirements. In addition, original titles of these works are changed to clearly present the main thesis and to explicitly indicate the author's opinion. Every effort is made to ensure that Greenhaven Publishing accurately reflects the original intent of the authors. Every effort has been made to trace the owners of the copyrighted material.

Cover image: Howard Davies/Corbis Documentary/Getty Images
Map: frees/Shutterstock.com

Library of Congress Cataloging-in-Publication Data

Names: Wiener, Gary, editor.
Title: Anti-semitism and the boycott, divestment, and sanctions movement / Gary Wiener, book editor.
Other titles: Global viewpoints.
Description: New York : Greenhaven Publishing, 2019. | Series: Global viewpoints | Includes bibliographical references and index. | Audience: 9–12.
Identifiers: LCCN 2018025860| ISBN 9781534503908 (library bound) | ISBN 9781534504677 (pbk.)
Subjects: LCSH: Boycott Divestment and Sanctions (Movement) | Arab-Israeli conflict. | Palestinian Arabs—Civil rights. | Boycotts—Israel. | Disinvestment—Israel. | Economic sanctions—Israel. | Antisemitism—Israel.
Classification: LCC DS119.76 .A66 2019 | DDC 956.9405/5—dc23
LC record available at https://lccn.loc.gov/2018025860

Manufactured in the United States of America

Website: http://greenhavenpublishing.com

Contents

Chapter 2: Is the BDS Movement Justified and Effective?

Chapter 4: Is BDS Anti-Semitic?

Foreword

*"The problems of all of humanity can
only be solved by all of humanity."*
—Swiss author Friedrich Dürrenmatt

Global interdependence has become an undeniable reality. Mass media and technology have increased worldwide access to information and created a society of global citizens. Understanding and navigating this global community is a challenge, requiring a high degree of information literacy and a new level of learning sophistication.

Building on the success of its flagship series, Opposing Viewpoints, Greenhaven Publishing has created the Global Viewpoints series to examine a broad range of current, often controversial topics of worldwide importance from a variety of international perspectives. Providing students and other readers with the information they need to explore global connections and think critically about worldwide implications, each Global Viewpoints volume offers a panoramic view of a topic of widespread significance.

Drugs, famine, immigration—a broad, international treatment is essential to do justice to social, environmental, health, and political issues such as these. Junior high, high school, and early college students, as well as general readers, can all use Global Viewpoints anthologies to discern the complexities relating to each issue. Readers will be able to examine unique national perspectives while, at the same time, appreciating the interconnectedness that global priorities bring to all nations and cultures.

Material in each volume is selected from a diverse range of sources, including journals, magazines, newspapers, nonfiction books, speeches, government documents, pamphlets, organization newsletters, and position papers. Global Viewpoints is truly global, with material drawn primarily from international sources available in English and secondarily from US sources with extensive international coverage.

Features of each volume in the Global Viewpoints series include:

- An **annotated table of contents** that provides a brief summary of each essay in the volume, including the name of the country or area covered in the essay.

- An **introduction** specific to the volume topic.

- A **world map** to help readers locate the countries or areas covered in the essays.

- For each viewpoint, an **introduction** that contains notes about the author and source of the viewpoint explains why material from the specific country is being presented, summarizes the main points of the viewpoint, and offers three **guided reading questions** to aid in understanding and comprehension.

- **For further discussion questions** that promote critical thinking by asking the reader to compare and contrast aspects of the viewpoints or draw conclusions about perspectives and arguments.

- A worldwide list of **organizations to contact** for readers seeking additional information.

- A **periodical bibliography** for each chapter and a **bibliography of books** on the volume topic to aid in further research.

- A comprehensive **subject index** to offer access to people, places, events, and subjects cited in the text.

Global Viewpoints is designed for a broad spectrum of readers who want to learn more about current events, history, political science, government, international relations, economics, environmental science, world cultures, and sociology—students doing research for class assignments or debates, teachers and faculty seeking to supplement course materials, and others wanting to understand current issues better. By presenting how people in various countries perceive the root causes, current consequences, and proposed solutions to worldwide challenges, Global Viewpoints volumes offer readers opportunities to enhance their global awareness and their knowledge of cultures worldwide.

Introduction

> *"Today, there are a similar number of Jews and Palestinians living between the Jordan River and the Mediterranean Sea. They have a choice. They can choose to live together in one state, or they can separate into two states. But here is a fundamental reality: if the choice is one state, Israel can either be Jewish or democratic – it cannot be both – and it won't ever really be at peace. Moreover, the Palestinians will never fully realize their vast potential in a homeland of their own with a one-state solution."*
>
> —*US Secretary of State John Kerry, December 28, 2016*

In Late 2017, a seventeen-year old Palestinian girl named Ahed Tamimi was arrested after a video surfaced showing her slapping and kicking Israeli soldiers. The incident occurred in the occupied West Bank, an area east of Israel that has almost three million people, 2.7 million of whom are Palestinians. The territory was captured during the 1967 war. Tamimi said she was angered that her fifteen-year-old cousin had been wounded in a clash with Israeli troops. In March of 2018, Tamimi accepted a plea bargain that had her serving eight months in prison. Despite the plea bargain, Tamimi has stated that "there is no justice and we are in an illegal court."[1] The case has made Tamimi a Palestinian hero and serves as an exemplar of the continuing tensions between Palestinians and Israelis.

The ongoing dispute between the Palestinians and Israel has raged since the 1948 formation of the Jewish homeland. Palestinians have sought many methods of attacking Israel, including launching missiles, digging tunnels into the country, and inciting terrorist attacks, including suicide bombings. By contrast, the Boycott, Divest, and Sanctions Movement (BDS) is a peaceful, nonviolent campaign, but its application has much further reaching implications for Israel than the random violence of past attacks. Many Palestinians believe that BDS will force Israel to grant them independence. Many Israelis believe that BDS threatens Israel's survival as a Jewish state.

The Boycott, Divestment, and Sanctions Movement was founded in July 2005 by 170 Palestinian nongovernmental organizations. The campaign was organized and coordinated by the Palestinian BDS National Committee. According to its website, "The Boycott, Divestment, Sanctions (BDS) movement works to end international support for Israel's oppression of Palestinians and pressure Israel to comply with international law."[2] Inspired by the South African anti-apartheid movement, part of which included a worldwide boycott of the African nation, the Palestinian BDS campaign exhorts other nations to exert nonviolent pressure on Israel until it meets the following three demands:

1. Ending its occupation and colonization of all Arab lands and dismantling the Wall.

2. Recognizing the fundamental rights of the Arab-Palestinian citizens of Israel to full equality.

3. Respecting, protecting, and promoting the rights of Palestinian refugees to return to their homes and properties as stipulated in UN Resolution 194.[3]

For their part, many Israelis feel the comparison of their situation to Apartheid is inaccurate and unfair.

Omar Barghouti, a founding member of BDS, has become

something of the face of BDS and its leading spokesperson. Unlike many in the international community, Barghouti does not favor a two state solution, in which Israelis and Palestinians would have their own separate countries. Instead, he believes in the Palestinian right to return to the now-Israeli territory from which many of their families were displaced by war in the twentieth century. Barghouti is very clear, and has always been explicit, about what he expects from the BDS movement. His master plan, which the Israelis might label a scheme, is ultimately to have Arabs in Israel outnumber Jews, and use these numbers to vote out the Israeli regime. In an interview, Barghouti has stated, "People fighting for refugee rights like I am, know that you cannot reconcile the right of return for refugees with a two state solution. That is the big white elephant in the room and people are ignoring it—a return for refugees would end Israel's existence as a Jewish state."[4]

Clearly, Barghouti's plan poses an existential threat to the survival of Israel as a Jewish homeland. As Sharon Nazarian of the Anti-Defamation League writes, "The right of return for Palestinian refugees would mean the de-facto end of the Jewish state, so as a starting point for negotiations, it demands as a precursor the end of Israel."[5] It is no wonder, then, that so many Jews in Israel and abroad are opposed to BDS.

Writing for *Commentary* magazine, Efraim Karsh expounds on the one-state solution that the success of BDS would create: "During the past decade or so, the actual elimination of the Jewish state has become a *cause célèbre* among many of these educated Westerners," Karsh writes. He goes on:

> The "one-state solution," as it is called, is a euphemistic formula proposing the replacement of Israel by a state, theoretically comprising the whole of historic Palestine, in which Jews will be reduced to the status of a permanent minority. Only this, it is said, can expiate the "original sin" of Israel's founding, an act built (in the words of one critic) "on the ruins of Arab Palestine" and achieved through the deliberate and aggressive dispossession of its native population.[6]

Uri Avnery, Israeli writer and founder of the *Gush Shalom* peace movement, notes that the one-state solution is highly impractical, given the centuries-old antipathy between the two peoples: "Here we have two fiercely nationalistic peoples," he observes, "who claim the same homeland. Will they live peacefully in one common state? Life would be hell in such a state." Avnery references an Israeli joke: "Can the wolf live with the lamb? No problem. But you have to give the wolf a new lamb every day."[7]

Barghouti and those of like mind may be serious about their one-state proposal, but there are good reasons why the rest of the world is unlikely to let that happen. Extrapolating the ultimate BDS scenario out to a Palestinian-controlled Israel must take into account the reality that Israel is a nuclear state that has had atomic weaponry since the 1960s. If the United States and its allies are loathe to allow a nuclear Iran, and have worked to de-escalate tensions with a nuclear North Korea, there is little possibility that these superpowers would allow a nuclear Palestine. Consider that currently the Palestinian Gaza Strip is controlled by Hamas, an organization that the United States and the European Union both regard as a terrorist group. Allowing a Hamas-controlled nuclear Palestine might push the symbolic doomsday clock (which now registers about two minutes to an apocalyptic midnight) even closer to human extinction.

All of this is not to say that Israel, as currently led by Benjamin Netanyahu, is perfect or blameless. Protecting Israel's borders, security, economics, and academics from BDS are necessary steps that any country must pursue when under attack. But many liberal Jews, in Israel and abroad, have taken issue with Netanyahu's perceived overzealous persecution of the Palestinians. Many have sided with the Palestinians over Netanyahu's right-wing government. But Israel is a free country, a democracy, and voters have consistently sided with Netanyahu in the last several elections. Fear is a powerful motivator, and Israel is surrounded by enemies.

Tensions between Palestinians and Israelis have recently been amplified by President Trump's decision to move the American embassy from Tel Aviv to Jerusalem. Palestinians have protested, angrily, fearing that Trump's move will cement Jerusalem, the city they believe is their capitol, as an Israeli stronghold. With Trump obviously favoring Israel's claims over those of the Palestinians, fuel has been added to an already raging fire. It is likely that BDS will not be going away any time soon.

In principle, the BDS campaign officially opposes anti-Semitism. Its website states that "BDS is an inclusive, anti-racist human rights movement that is opposed on principle to all forms of discrimination, including anti-Semitism and Islamophobia."[8] Whether BDS activists uphold these practices in actuality is up for debate, however. The contributors in *Global Viewpoints: Anti-Semitism and the Boycott, Divestment, and Sanctions Movement* approach the conflict from many different perspectives. Both Israeli and Arab points of view are well represented, as are perspectives from the international community. Many of the viewpoints suggest how far apart the two sides are. Hopefully, open discussion of the issues will someday result in a resolution that all parties can agree upon.

Notes

1. "The Latest: Palestinian teenage protester gets 8 months." *The Associated Press.* March 21, 2018.
2. "What is BDS?" BDS. https://bdsmovement.net/what-is-bds
3. "What is BDS?" BDS. https://bdsmovement.net/what-is-bds
4. Ali Mustafa, "Boycotts Work: An Interview with Omar Barghouti." *The Electronic Intifada.* May 31, 2009.
5. Sharon Nazarian "By Rejecting Jews, Intersectionality Betrays Itself." *Forward.* January 25, 2018.
   https://forward.com/opinion/392901/by-rejecting-jews-intersectionality-betrays-itself/
6. Efraim Karsh, "1948, Israel, and the Palestinians—The True Story." *Commentary.* May 1, 2008. https://www.commentarymagazine.com/articles/1948-israel-and-the-palestinians-the-true-story/
7. Uri Avnery, "Why BDS Won't Save Us." *Haaretz.* Sept 18, 2017. https://www.haaretz.com/opinion/.premium-why-bds-wont-save-us-1.5451928
8. "What is BDS?" BDS. https://bdsmovement.net/what-is-bds

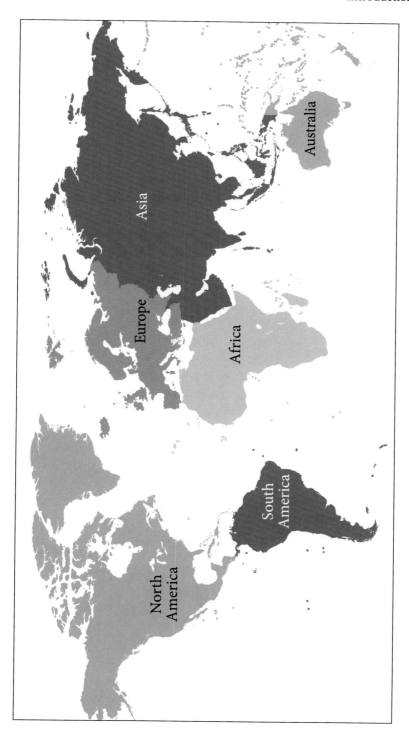

GLOBALVIEWPOINTS

CHAPTER

History of the Dispute Between Israel and the Palestinians

A History of the Israeli-Palestinian Conflict

Washington Report on Middle East Affairs

The following viewpoint presents an overview of the Israeli-Palestinian divide. Since 1948, when the British divided up Palestine into an Arab and a Jewish state, the conflict over this territory has been a heated one. Despite attempts by both sides to characterize the conflict as a religious and ethnic one, the real issue is one of territory: who controls it and who inhabits it. Progressive Israelis and Palestinians understand that there is hope for a peaceful resolution and that negotiations are a better alternative than violence. Washington Report on Middle East Affairs *is published eight times a year and focuses on news and analysis from and about the Middle East and US policy in that region. It claims to be a non-partisan publication but has been criticized as being aligned with the Arab lobby and as anti-Israel.*

As you read, consider the following questions:

1. How has the dispute over formerly Palestinian territory progressed since 1948?
2. Is this viewpoint nonpartisan, or does it seem to favor one side over another?
3. What solution do the authors offer for resolving the crisis?

"The Origins of the Israeli-Palestinian Conflict," Jews for Justice in the Middle East, IF AMERICANS KNEW. Reprinted by permission.

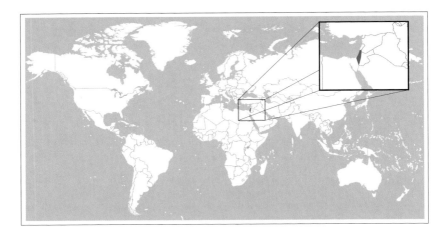

1948: The Origins of the Israeli-Palestinian Conflict

As in Ireland, India and Cyprus, British colonial "divide and rule" tactics culminated in November 1947 in the partition of Palestine into two newly independent states—one Palestinian Arab and one Jewish.

UN Resolution 181 allotted Jews, who were less than one-third of the population and owned only 8 percent of the land, 56 percent of the territory of Palestine. Palestinians saw the partition plan as a grave injustice, especially since most Jews in Palestine were recent arrivals. Fighting broke out between Jewish forces and local Palestinian militias.

In May 1948, the British evacuated Palestine, and Israel declared independence. Several adjacent Arab countries declared war against the new state. During the war, Israeli forces destroyed over 500 Palestinian villages and captured 78 percent of historic Palestine.

By the war's end, 70 percent of all Palestinians had been made refugees. In December 1948, the United Nations passed Resolution 194, stating that, "The refugees wishing to return to their homes and live at peace with their neighbors should be permitted to do so at the earliest practicable date...compensation should be paid for the property of those choosing not to return." But this resolution has never been implemented.

1967: Israeli Occupation—37 Years and Counting

In 1967, Israel occupied the West Bank, Gaza, East Jerusalem and the Syrian Golan Heights, putting Israel in possession of the remaining 22 percent of historic Palestine.

Israel tried to portray itself as a "benign occupier," but Palestinians demanded self-determination and statehood. In order to maintain its military rule, Israel has resorted to grave human rights violations including: deportation, land confiscation, house demolitions, the construction of settlements, arbitrary arrests, denial of due process and assassination of Palestinian leaders.

In 1987, Palestinians began a popular uprising, or Intifada, for self-determination in an independent Palestinian state.

1993: The Short-lived Hope of Peace

In 1993, the US brokered an agreement between the Israeli and Palestinian leaderships in Oslo, Norway. The Oslo Accords were intended as a framework to end the Israeli-Palestinian conflict. But the terms were so heavily weighted in Israel's favor that the Agreements enabled Israel to consolidate its control over the West Bank and Gaza under the banner of the "peace process."

Under Oslo, Israeli settlements have been expanded into large blocs and a massive road network (directly funded by US taxes) has been built exclusively for Israeli settlers — all in violation of the Fourth Geneva Convention. A maze of roadblocks and permanent military checkpoints is used to police Palestinian movement and to bar Palestinians from reaching their jobs, schools, hospitals and places of worship in Israel proper and Jerusalem. Israel controls all travel between the West Bank and Gaza, and the territories themselves have been truncated into a dozen isolated cantons, separated by Israeli-controlled areas. Large portions of Palestinian territory are still patrolled by Israeli soldiers and occupied by hostile settlers. In fact, the number of settlers doubled between 1993-2000. Palestinians are unable to move freely between their towns and villages or control their borders, economy or natural resources.

September 2000: the Second Palestinian Uprising

The failure of the peace process to guarantee basic Palestinian human rights and political independence fueled frustration and despair that ignited a second Palestinian Intifada in September 2000.

Israeli forces have responded to Palestinian demands for independence by attacking towns and villages with US-made Apache helicopters and F-16 fighter jets and using heavy weapons, including tanks, against civilians.

Palestinian communities are under siege:

- large areas are under 24-hour or dawn-to-dusk curfews;
- people cannot move between villages and towns and goods cannot be transported;
- schools and universities are closed;
- tanks and armored personnel carriers surround homes and neighborhoods;
- in some areas, food and fuel supplies have run dangerously low;
- vaccination programs and primary health care systems are frozen;
- sewage and garbage go uncollected, posing a public health threat;
- Israeli soldiers have denied passage to ambulances, even those carrying critical cases;
- dozens of Palestinians have died because they cannot reach hospitals;
- patients in need of kidney dialysis and cancer treatment cannot receive care;
- and numerous women have been forced to give birth at army checkpoints on the way to the hospital.

The US as an Obstacle to Peace

Although the US has claimed to be an "honest broker" between Israel and the Palestinians, it has provided the weapons, funding and political backing for Israel to maintain the occupation.

Weapons: US weapons transfers to Israel actually increased during the current crisis, with the decade's largest sale of Blackhawk and Apache attack helicopters. These have been used to fire antitank missiles into Palestinian homes, government offices, schools and hospitals.

Funding: US military aid to Israel has also increased, along with Israeli human rights violations. Israel has long been the single largest recipient of US foreign aid. The more than $3 billion in military and economic aid that Israel gets annually is nearly 40 percent of the entire US aid budget. Meanwhile, Israel represents only 0.1 percent of the world's population.

Political Backing: The US has used its veto on the Security Council of the United Nations to block nearly half of all UN resolutions condemning Israel for human rights abuses against Palestinians and violations of international law. Since September 2000, the Bush Administration has twice vetoed the creation of an international observer force to the region, a key demand of Palestinian and Israeli peace activists.

The US has clearly forfeited its role as a broker for peace. Future negotiations between Israel and the Palestinian leadership should therefore be held under the auspices of the United Nations, not the US, and all future agreements must meet standards of international human rights and humanitarian law.

Why Does the US Provide So Much Support for Israel?

Since World War Two, US policy in the Middle East has focused on securing access to the region's oil reserves, which are the richest in the world. Access to oil is defined as a matter of national security since the US economy and military depend on the flow of cheap oil.

As the designated "watchdog" of US interests in the Middle East, Israel's role has been twofold:

- to thwart the rise of political movements (like the secular Arab nationalism espoused by most Palestinians) that might jeopardize US access to oil. In the past, governments led by nationalists (e.g., Egypt under Nasser) have asserted that control over Middle East oil should be in the hands of the region's governments. Some have even talked about using oil revenues to benefit ordinary people in the Middle East instead of a small US and Arab elite.

- to dominate the Middle East militarily so that no government in the region can challenge US control of oil resources.

We often hear about Israel helping to "maintain stability" in the Middle East. For people in the region, that means preserving a status quo in which corrupt and undemocratic governments (like Saudi Arabia) reign unchallenged in exchange for granting the US access to oil. The big losers are ordinary people in the Middle East, who remain impoverished and without basic human rights.

Isn't the Israeli-Palestinian Conflict an Ancient Ethnic/Religious Rivalry?

Despite attempts on both sides to mobilize people on the basis of ethnic and religious identity, the conflict is fundamentally political: a dispute over territory, who controls it and who inhabits it.

Misconceptions about the nature of the Israeli-Palestinian conflict sometimes stem from the fact that Israel's representatives encourage a conflation between Zionism (Israeli nationalism) and Jewish identity. For example, Israeli leaders routinely claim to act "in the name of the Jewish People."

But Zionism is a political ideology, while Judaism is a religion and a cultural practice. Not all Jews are Zionists and not all Zionists are Jews.

The Modern Middle East

Towards the end of the 1800s questions arose as to how the Jewish people could overcome increasing persecution and anti-Semitism in Europe. The biblical Promised Land led to a political movement, Zionism, to establish a Jewish homeland in Palestine, in the Middle East.

From 1920 to 1947, the British Empire had a mandate over Palestine. At that time, Palestine included all of Israel and today's Occupied Territories, of Gaza, West Bank, etc. The increasing number of Jewish people immigrating to the Holy Land increased tensions in the region.

European geopolitics in the earlier half of the 20th century in the wider Middle East region contributed to a lot of instability overall. The British Empire, especially, played a major role in the region.

During World War I, in 1916, it convinced Arab leaders to revolt against the Ottoman Empire (which was allied with Germany). In return, the British government would support the establishment of an independent Arab state in the region, including Palestine.

Yet, in contradiction to this, and to also get support of Jewish people, in 1917, Lord Arthur Balfour, then British Foreign Minister, issued a declaration (the Balfour Declaration). This announced the British Empire's support for the establishment of a Jewish national home in Palestine.

As a further complication, there was a deal between Imperial Britain and France to carve up the Arab provinces of the Ottoman Empire and divide control of the region. The spoils of war were to be shared. As with the 1885 Berlin Conference where Africa was carved up amongst the various European empires, parts of the Middle East were also to be carved up, which would require artificial borders, support of monarchies, dictators and other leaders that could be regarded as puppets or at least could be influenced by these external powers.

"The Middle East Conflict—a Brief Background," by Anup Shah, Global Issues,
July 30, 2006.

Palestinian Children on the Front Lines

Palestinian youth have played a key role in confronting Israeli troops in the West Bank and Gaza. In the US, some mainstream media has uncritically echoed Israeli claims that Palestinians deliberately place their children in front of Israeli troops in order to profit politically from media images of Israeli brutality. This is an unfounded accusation that blames Palestinians for their own deaths and presumes that Palestinian parents willingly sacrifice their children's lives. The notion that these parents protect or love their children any less than other mothers and fathers reflects the dehumanization of Palestinians in the US media. It is always disturbing to see children engaged in political turmoil created by adults. Yet their participation in the conflict should be understood in a historical context. Youth have been on the front lines of demonstrations for national independence and struggles for social justice worldwide. Children killed by South African police at Sharpsville and Soweto and those attacked by US police during civil rights protests were, like Palestinian youth today, considered heroes who were fighting for a better future for themselves and their community. The real question is not why so many young people are protesting, but why the Israeli military is reacting to stone-throwing youth with live ammunition and antitank missiles.

On Media Bias

US headlines and opinion pieces have presented a false symmetry between Israelis and Palestinians in the current confrontations. The reality is that one of the world's best equipped armies is confronting mostly young, unarmed stone-throwers with massive military force. Yet most media coverage in the US would lead us to think that two equal forces are confronting each other. Some US media have gone so far as to imply that Palestinian civilians are the aggressors and the Israeli army an embattled underdog. We see this inversion of reality in statements like that of former US Secretary of State Madeleine Albright, who remarked at the beginning of the uprising that Palestinians have "placed Israel under siege" and that the Israeli army is defending itself (NBC's "Meet the Press,"10/8/00). Comments like Albright's simply ignore Israel's 34-year, illegal occupation and the litany of human rights violations that have accompanied the occupation. To ignore the occupation is to erase both the context and the content of Palestinian grievances, making it seem as though Palestinians are protesting for no reason. Armed attacks by Palestinian groups are similarly presented without any context and with no reference to Israeli violence. Usually, Palestinian attacks are portrayed as arbitrary and unprovoked incidents, while Israeli military violence is portrayed as purely retaliatory.

What Is Washington Report on Middle East Affairs's Position on the Israeli-Palestinian Conflict?

As in other national conflicts, international law and international human rights standards must be respected by all parties and should serve as a basis for finding a solution.

That means that Israel is accountable to the same human rights standards as all governments and is obligated to:

- Withdraw fully and unconditionally from all of the territories occupied in 1967;

- Comply with United Nations resolutions aimed at resolving the conflict, including:

  - UN Resolution 242, mandating an Israeli withdrawal from the West Bank, Gaza and East Jerusalem;

  - UN Resolution 338, calling for negotiations to establish "a just and durable peace in the Middle East";

  - UN Resolution 194, providing the legal foundation for the right of return of Palestinian refugees.

- And end policies that discriminate against Palestinian citizens of Israel.

The Palestinian leadership and other Palestinian factions are also accountable to international standards of human rights and humanitarian law. That means:

- An end to the targeting of Israeli civilians. Violence against civilians, whether perpetrated by Israeli or Palestinian forces, is a grave violation of human rights that must be opposed;

- The promotion of democratic policies and institutions within Palestinian society, including an end to policies that discriminate against women.

Is There Any Hope for Resolving the Israeli-Palestinian Conflict?

Yes! Fair-minded and realistic proposals for ending the occupation and resolving the core issues of the conflict have been put forward by progressive Palestinians and Israelis. Washington Report on Middle East Affairs's partners and friends in the region are those Palestinians and Israelis who are working toward coexistence based on equal rights.

Progressive Palestinians and Israelis understand that negotiations are the only alternative to violence. Many of them reject the terms of the Oslo Agreement, which was forced on Palestinians by Israel and the US. Instead, peace activists are calling for talks geared toward a just and sustainable settlement that can achieve peace and security for both peoples.

The Movement to Boycott Israel Has a Long History

Mitchell Bard

In the following viewpoint, Mitchell Bard examines how the current BDS boycott has roots dating back to just after World War I, when Arab nations instituted economic sanctions against what they referred to as "Zionists." The boycott was intended to isolate Israel from the surrounding Arab nations and the world community and to deny it trade that might be used to enhance its military and economic strength. The boycott has evolved over time, weakening and strengthening, and has been opposed by the United States. The boycott has been somewhat effective, but it has not completely curtailed Israel's economic and military growth. Bard is an American foreign policy analyst, editor, and author. His work focuses on US–Middle East policy. Bard is the Executive Director of the nonprofit American–Israeli Cooperative Enterprise (AICE), and the director of the Jewish Virtual Library. His many books include Death to the Infidels: Radical Islam's War Against the Jews.

As you read, consider the following questions:

1. What are the beginnings of the Arab movement to boycott Israel?
2. What are the three components of the original boycott?
3. How has the original boycott evolved over time?

"Arab League Boycott: Background & Overview," by Mitchell Bard, American-Israeli Cooperative Enterprise, February 2017. Reprinted by permission.

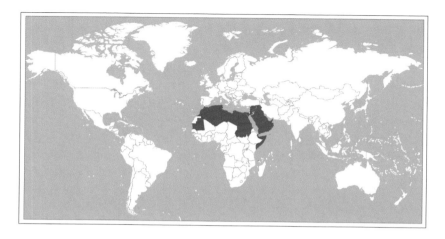

T he Arab boycott was formally declared by the newly formed Arab League Council on December 2, 1945:

> Jewish products and manufactured goods shall be considered undesirable to the Arab countries." All Arab "institutions, organizations, merchants, commission agents and individuals" were called upon "to refuse to deal in, distribute, or consume Zionist products or manufactured goods.

As is evident in this declaration, the terms "Jewish" and "Zionist" were used synonymously by the Arabs. Thus, even before the establishment of Israel, the Arab states had declared an economic boycott against the Jews of Palestine.

Overview

The boycott, as it evolved after 1948, is divided into three components. The primary boycott prohibits direct trade between Israel and the Arab nations. The secondary boycott is directed at companies that do business with Israel. The tertiary boycott involves the blacklisting of firms that trade with other companies that do business with Israel.

The blacklisting process is capricious; it is unclear whether boycott officials collect any evidence at all before placing an individual or company on the blacklist. No two countries have identical lists, and six countries — Algeria, Mauritania, Morocco, Somalia, the Sudan and Tunisia — do not enforce the secondary boycott. Egypt's policy changed from strict enforcement to unofficial complicity after the signing of the peace treaty with Israel, despite the provision whereby Egypt agreed to the "termination of economic boycotts and discriminatory barriers to the free movement of people and goods. . . ."

Once on the list, it is sometimes difficult to get off, since the company or some Arab sponsor must initiate the request. A firm might be required to supply proof that it no longer has any business with Israel and/or might be asked to make investments in Arab countries equal to those made earlier in Israel. Bribery is another means of becoming "de-listed."

The objective of the boycott has been to isolate Israel from its neighbors and the international community, as well as to deny it trade that might be used to augment its military and economic strength. Israel's capacity to reach its full economic potential was hindered for decades by the actions of Great Britain, Japan and other countries that cooperated with the boycott. It has undoubtedly enhanced Israel's isolation and separated the Jewish State from its most natural markets, but the boycott failed to undermine Israel's economy to the degree intended.

America Fights the Boycott

In 1977, Congress prohibited US companies from cooperating with the Arab boycott. When President Carter signed the law, he said the "issue goes to the very heart of free trade among nations" and that it was designed to "end the divisive effects on American life of foreign boycotts aimed at Jewish members of our society."

The Arab League threatened to take a decisive stand against the new law, which was regarded as part of "a campaign of hysterical laws and bills . . . which Israel and world Zionism are trying not only to enforce on the US; but also in some countries of Western Europe."

Contrary to claims that the bill would lead to a drastic reduction in American trade with the Arab world, imports and exports increased substantially. Broader diplomatic and cultural relations also improved. Nevertheless, certain US companies were blacklisted for their relations with Israel. In addition, few other nations adopted anti-boycott laws and, instead, complied with the boycott. For example, the Military Aircraft Division of British Aerospace sent a purchase order to an American supplier in connection with the British agreement to sell Saudi Arabia Tornado aircraft and other weapons in the late 1980's. It guaranteed none of the items "are made in Israel directly or indirectly either in whole or in part and such items are not reshipped from Israel for Israeli account or by proxy for or on behalf of or with any persons or organizations resident in Israel. The supplier moreover warrants not to dispatch any of the items on any Israeli carrier."

For many years, language has been included in the foreign operations appropriations acts concerning the boycott. For example, Section 535 of the Foreign Operations, Export Financing, and Related Programs Appropriations Act, 2006 (P.L. 109-102), states that: (1) it is the sense of Congress that the Arab League boycott is an impediment to peace in the region and to United States investment and trade in the region; (2) the boycott should be revoked and the CBO disbanded; (3) all Arab League states should normalize relations with Israel; and (4) the President and the Secretary of State should continue vigorously to oppose the boycott and encourage Arab states to assume normal trading relations with Israel. US embassies and government officials raise the boycott with host country officials, noting the persistence of illegal boycott requests and the impact on both US firms and on the countries' ability to expand trade and investment.

In August 2007, the federal antiboycott statutes were revised amending the existing penalty guidelines and outlining procedures for firms to voluntarily report violations of the law. Officials hope that by providing companies an incentive to "come clean " they will do so and save the Commerce Department the need for costly investigations.

The Boycott Begins to Crack

On September 30, 1994, the six Gulf Cooperation Council states announced they would no longer support the secondary boycott barring trade with companies doing business with Israel, but US companies continued as of 2007 to receive requests to cooperate with the boycott from GCC countries. At a meeting in Taba, Egypt, February 7-8, 1995, Egyptian, American, Jordanian and Palestinian trade leaders signed a joint document — the Taba Declaration-supporting "all efforts to end the boycott of Israel."

Since the signing of peace agreements between Israel and the PLO and Jordan, the boycott has gradually crumbled. The Arab League was forced to cancel several boycott meetings called by the Syrian hosts because of opposition from countries like Kuwait, Morocco and Tunisia. The primary boycott — prohibiting direct relations between Arab countries and Israel — has slowly cracked as nations like Qatar, Oman and Morocco have negotiated deals with Israel. Furthermore, few countries outside the Middle East continue to comply with the boycott. Japan, for example, has exponentially increased its trade with Israel since the peace process began. Still, the boycott remains technically in force and several countries continue its enforcement (e.g., Lebanon enforces the primary, secondary and tertiary boycotts).

Into the New Millennium

In April 2004, representatives from 19 Arab countries met for the 72nd conference Bureau for Boycotting Israel to discuss tightening the boycott. The four-day meeting considered blacklisting new companies that do business with the Jewish state. Mauritania, Egypt and Jordan, which have diplomatic ties with Israel, stayed away from the meeting.

In late 2005, Saudi Arabia was required to cease its boycott of Israel as a condition of joining the World Trade Organization. After initially saying that it would do so, the government subsequently announced it would maintain its first-degree boycott of Israeli products. The government said it agreed to lift the second and third degree boycott in accordance with an earlier Gulf Cooperation Council decision rather than the demands of the WTO. In June 2006, the Saudi ambassador admitted his country still enforced the boycott in violation of promises made earlier to the Bush Administration and the Saudis participated in the 2007 boycott conference.

During free trade agreement negotiations with Bahrain, Oman and the United Arab Emirates, the status of the boycott was an issue of concern and the countries agreed not to comply with the boycott. However, indications suggest that these countries continue to support the boycott.

Representatives from only 14 Arab countries attended the biannual conference of the Arab League's Bureau for Boycotting Israel in Syria in April 2007. Mauritania, Egypt, Jordan, Bahrain and Oman were among the nations that were absent. Those that did participate included the Palestinian Authority, Lebanon, Saudi Arabia and Iraq.

The US government has raised concerns about the enforcement of the boycott by Iraq. In 2006, the number of requests from Iraq for US companies to comply with the boycott increased 287%. Requests in 2006 were also up from Lebanon, Bahrain and Qatar. The largest source of boycott-related requests comes from the United Arab Emirates. In 2006, according to the Department of Commerce, nine companies paid just under $96,000 to settle allegations that they violated the US antiboycott provisions, an increase from five cases in 2005 and $57,000. In January 2007, the New York office of the National Bank of Egypt was fined $22,500 for boycott violations.

BDS

Today, most Arab countries publicly support the boycott even as several quietly trade with Israel. One reason has been US pressure for these countries to normalize relations. Beyond the Arab League boycott, an additional boycott campaign was launched in 2001 aimed at isolating Israel and, ultimately, making it disappear with the help of international sanctions. This boycott, divestment and sanctions (BDS) movement has spread around the world. Various countries, including Spain, France and the United Kingdom, have taken measures to outlaw aspects of the campaign. Legislation at the Federal level is still being developed to combat BDS. Congress, for example, has called on negotiators in trade talks with the European Union discourage politically motivated economic actions intended to penalize or otherwise limit commercial relations specifically with Israel or person doing business in Israel or in Israeli controlled territories.

The BDS movement has been adopted by anti-Israel organizations on a number of college campuses, some of which have attempted to convince their universities to divest from US companies doing business in Israel. Even on the few campuses where student government passed divestment resolutions, the university administrations have made clear they have no intention of boycotting Israel.

Another campus-led phenomenon involved faculty who have lobbied professional associations to boycott Israel. Curiously, these faculty insist on their academic freedom to call for a boycott against Israel, but deny their critics the right to speak out against them. They also see no hypocrisy in denying Israelis their academic freedom. The Modern Language Association and American Studies Association were two of the groups that voted to boycott Israel. The decisions had no practical effect since the associations themselves do not have relations with Israel and the only members who adhere to the boycott are those who had no interest in visiting Israel or working with Israeli colleagues. Those decisions to boycott Israel also provoked a backlash against faculty and associations supporting BDS. The American Studies Association decision, for example, was condemned by more than 200 university presidents/chancellors. More esteemed associations, such as the American Historical Association, have rejected efforts to put a boycott on their agenda.

The backlash has extended off campus as well where state legislatures have adopted legislation aimed at preventing any boycott of Israel.

The Massacre at Deir Yassin Has Come to Symbolize the Palestinian Plight

Catrina Stewart

In the following viewpoint, Catrina Stewart focuses on Deir Yassin, an Arab village in which a brutal battle was fought between Jewish forces and Palestinians in 1948, just weeks before Israel was formed. What actually happened in Deir Yassin is subject to interpretation. Palestinians claim it was cleared out in what has now come to be called ethnic cleansing. Israelis claim that the Arabs died in a fierce battle with their forces. Israel has been loathe to release documents relating to Deir Yassin for fear that they might incite Palestinian violence and worldwide condemnation. Many historians cite Deir Yassin as the catalyst that led to the flight of 750,000 Palestinians. Deir Yassin has come to symbolize the Palestinian notion of dispossession. Stewart is a British freelance journalist. She has been based in Moscow, the Middle East, and East Africa, and has written for the AP, the Independent, *and others.*

As you read, consider the following questions:

1. What is the significance of Deir Yassin to Israeli-Palestinian relations?
2. What do documents from that era seem to show about what happened at Deir Yassin?
3. Why do Israelis and Palestinians have such differing opinions on what occurred at Deir Yassin?

"A Massacre of Arabs Masked by a State of National Amnesia," by Catrina Stewart, The Independent, May 9, 2010. Reprinted by permission.

More than one unwitting visitor to Jerusalem has fallen prey to the bizarre delusion that they are the Messiah. Usually, they are whisked off to the serene surroundings of Kfar Shaul psychiatric hospital on the outskirts of the city, where they are gently nursed back to health.

It is an interesting irony that the patients at Kfar Shaul recuperate from such variations on amnesia on the very spot that Israel has sought to erase from its collective memory.

The place is Deir Yassin. An Arab village cleared out in 1948 by Jewish forces in a brutal battle just weeks before Israel was formed, Deir Yassin has come to symbolise perhaps more than anywhere else the Palestinian sense of dispossession.

Sixty-two years on, what really happened at Deir Yassin on 9 April remains obscured by lies, exaggerations and contradictions. Now *Ha'aretz*, a liberal Israeli newspaper, is seeking to crack open the mystery by petitioning Israel's High Court of Justice to release written and photographic evidence buried deep in military archives. Palestinian survivors of Deir Yassin, a village of around 400 inhabitants, claim the Jews committed a wholesale massacre there, spurring Palestinians to flee in the thousands, and undermining the long-held Israeli narrative that they left of their own accord.

Israel's opposing version contends that Deir Yassin was the site of a pitched battle after Jewish forces faced unexpectedly strong resistance from the villagers. All of the casualties, it is argued, died in combat.

In 2006, an Israeli arts student, Neta Shoshani, applied for access to the Deir Yassin archives for a university project, believing a 50-year embargo on the secret documents had expired eight years previously. She was granted limited access to the material, but was informed that there was an extended ban on the more sensitive documents. When a lawyer demanded an explanation, it emerged that a ministerial committee only extended the ban more than a year after Ms Shoshani's first request, exposing the state to a legal challenge. The current embargo runs until 2012.

Defending its right to keep the documents under wraps, the Israeli state has argued that their publication would tarnish the country's image abroad and inflame Arab-Israeli tensions. Ha'aretz and Ms Shoshani have countered that the public have a right to know and confront their past.

Judges, who have viewed all the archived evidence held by the Israeli state on Deir Yassin, have yet to make a decision on what, if anything, to release. Among the documents believed to be in the state's possession is a damning report written by Meir Pa'il, a Jewish officer who condemned his compatriots for bloodthirsty and shameful conduct on that day. Equally incriminating are the many photographs that survive.

"The photos clearly show there was a massacre," says Daniel McGowan, a US retired professor who works with Deir Yassin Remembered. "Those photos show [villagers] lined up against a quarry wall and shot."

In 1947, the United Nations proposed a partition plan that would divide Palestine into a Jewish and Arab state, with Jerusalem an international city. The Arabs fiercely opposed the plan and clashes broke out as both sides scrambled for territory before the British mandate expired. In April 1948, the Hagana, the predecessor of the Israeli army, launched a military operation to secure safe passage between Jewish areas by taking Arab villages on high ground above the road to Jerusalem.

Irgun and the Stern Gang, breakaway paramilitary groups, drew up separate plans to take the strategic Deir Yassin in a pre-dawn raid on 9 April 1948, even though the villagers had signed a non-aggression pact with the Jews and had stuck to it. What happened next is still under debate. In his book *The Revolt*, Menachim Begin, a future Israeli prime minister, recounts how the Jewish forces used a loudspeaker to warn all the villagers to leave the village. Those that remained fought.

"Our men were compelled to fight for every house; to overcome the enemy they used large numbers of hand grenades," wrote Mr Begin, who was not present at the battle. "And the civilians who had disregarded our warnings suffered inevitable casualties. I am convinced that our officers and men wished to avoid a single unnecessary casualty."

Mr Begin's account, however, is challenged by the recollections of survivors and eyewitnesses. Abdul-Kader Zidain was 22 years old in 1948, and immediately joined a band of 30 fighters from the village to fend off the surprise Jewish offensive, even though they were clearly outnumbered.

"They went into the houses and they shot the people inside. They killed everybody they saw, women and children," said Mr Zidain, who lost four of his immediate family, including his father and two brothers, in the attack. Now a frail 84-year-old living in a West Bank village, he says he remembers everything as if it were yesterday. Survivor testimonies are supported by Mr Pa'il, whose detailed eyewitness account was published in 1998. Awaiting reassignment, he went to observe the attack as part of his remit to keep the Irgun and the Stern Gang in check.

After the fighting had wound down, Mr Pa'il described how he heard sporadic firing from the houses, and went to investigate. There he saw that the soldiers had stood the villagers in the corners of their homes and shot them dead. A short while later, he saw a group of around 25 prisoners being led to a quarry between Deir Yassin and neighbouring Givat Shaul. From a higher vantage point, he and a companion were able to see everything and take photographs. "There was a natural wall there, formed by diggingy. They stood the prisoners against that wall and shot the lot of them," he said. Mr Pa'il described how Jews from neighbouring Givat Shaul finally stepped in to stop the slaughter.

In the ensuing confusion and anger over the killings in Deir Yassin, both sides released an inflated Palestinian death toll for very different reasons: the Palestinians wanted to bolster resistance and attract the attention of the Arab nations they hoped would help them; the Jews wanted to scare the Palestinians into flight.

After the dust had settled, Mr Zidain and the other survivors counted the missing among them, and concluded that

105 Palestinians had died in Deir Yassin, not the 250 often reported. Four Jews were killed. But the damage was already done. The reports from Deir Yassin led to a total collapse of morale, and many historians regard the incident as the single biggest catalyst for the Palestinians' flight. By UN estimates, 750,000 Palestinians had fled their homes by the end of the 1948 War of Independence, roughly 60 per cent of Palestine's pre-war Arab population.

Mention Deir Yassin these days to most young Israelis and it will fail to register. Not far from the Kfar Shaul hospital, two teenage boys shake their heads at a question on Deir Yassin. Never heard of it, they say.

"Most Israelis treat the subject with total silence," says Professor McGowan. "They no longer deny it, they just don't talk about it."

The decision on whether that silence will now be broken remains in the hands of Israel's courts. "This was a big and important event in our history here. It was the first village we took and has a lot of meaning in the war that came after," says Ms Shoshani. "We have to deal with our past for our own sake."

There Was No Massacre at Deir Yassin

Shimon Cohen

In the following viewpoint, Shimon Cohen reviews the information presented in Professor Eliezer Tauber's book, Deir Yassin: The End of the Myth, *to argue that there was no massacre at the site. Professor Tauber sought out testimony from actual named participants in the Deir Yassin conflict, as opposed to others who cited only partisan sources. According to Tauber, the need for propaganda led Palestinians to exaggerate the story and promote the idea of a massacre. One Palestinian Tauber interviewed for his book noted that while the Jews are innocent of mass executions, the Arabs have still lost their land. Cohen is the founder and chairman of The PR Office, a Public Relations Consultancy that specializes in the Jewish community and nonprofit sector. He writes for The Jewish News Online and Israel National News, among other publications. He describes himself as a "spin consultant."*

As you read, consider the following questions:

1. Why does the 2017 book, *Deir Yassin: The End of the Myth*, claim there was no massacre at Dar Yassin?
2. What does Professor Tauber claim that the strategies he used to investigated Dar Yessin are superior to those of other writers?
3. Given the information presented, do the Israeli claims of innocence sound credible?

"There Was No Massacre at Deir Yassin," by Shimon Cohen, Arutz Sheva, July 18, 2017. Reprinted by permission.

I n his new book, *Deir Yassin: The End of the Myth*, Prof. Eliezer Tauber, head of the Institute for the Study of Underground Movements at Bar-Ilan University and former Dean of the Faculty of Jewish Studies at the University, examines the events of that day in April 1948 when the Arab village of Deir Yassin was attacked by Lehi and Etzel (Irgun or IZL) fighters, and reveals step by step the origin of the myth that a massacre was committed against the villagers.

Prof. Tauber opened his recent interview with Arutz Sheva by highlighting the central conclusion of his book.

"Basically there was no massacre in Deir Yassin."

In explaining what led him to that conclusion, Tauber noted that, since the Israeli-Arab conflict by definition consists of both Israelis and Arabs, it is not possible to reach real conclusions regarding the issues related to it without carefully examining the claims of both sides. This is in contrast to previous writers who examined the Deir Yassin affair by investigating only one side of those involved in the incident.

To write his book, Tauber thus turned to both Jewish and Arab sources, to the testimonies of Etzel (Irgun) and Lehi fighters, and to the testimonies of the Arabs at the scene. Not surprisingly, he said, the testimonies sound similar and express the same conclusion: There was no massacre at Deir Yassin.

The data collection process for the book included locating documents and recorded interviews conducted by the parties over the years, as well as interviews with some of those involved in the affair who are still alive.

According to Tauber, interviews with Arab refugees show an amazing picture that disproves the supposed massacre attributed to underground fighters by politically motivated parties who were not present at the event itself but addressed it later.

Prof. Tauber said that, at the beginning of his work, he embarked on a mission that was considered by many to be impossible - to locate each and every one of the Arabs present at the incident or who died during it, to identify all of them by name and not simply relate to them as "a bunch of Arabs," and to understand the reasons for the death of each one, investigate these reasons and thereby gain a complete picture of the incident.

"When you understand how each one died, you can understand what happened there," he said, asserting that the historians who later spread the rumors of a massacre "had no idea of what happened in Deir Yassin."

In this context, he mentioned the description in Haaretz according to which the incident involved a few defenseless villagers. "They don't know anything about the village because they based their claims on sources that were not at the scene," he said, noting that in reality, "the village was fortified. There is a list of guard positions and more. A delegation from the village went to Egypt to obtain weapons. Weapons arrived five days before the attack, a result of totally random timing. Egyptian intelligence arrested them because they bought the weapons on the black market," he said, noting that "if the weapons had not reached the village, all [the Arab villagers] would have fled, and not only 70 percent of them."

Prof. Tauber went on to present a number of examples showing the intensive level of investigation he conducted. Among other things, he told of a moment during the event when Etzel (Irgun) men knocked on the door of a house containing a woman and five men, one of whom was holding a rifle.

The woman came out, and she is the one who survived and related the incident. Afterward, the man with the rifle came out, and when the Jewish fighters noticed the rifle, they threw a grenade, and the five men were killed.

Prof. Tauber argues that, based on familiarity with the Arab mentality, the man with the rifle came out to surrender, but the choice to come out with the rifle instead of throwing it down misled the Etzel fighters. The significance is that, while there was no real danger to the Etzel fighters, at the time it was impossible to know this, and their response was appropriate in light of what they perceived was happening.

"If anyone defines this as a 'massacre,' I have nothing to say to him," Tauber said, adding that "At that time a procedure was very common whereby the [Jewish] soldiers surrounded their wounded with women so they would not be shot at, but the Arab snipers continued to shoot and hit the women. I am not arguing about ethics. My book is not a book of ethics but one about historical truth."

So, then, how did the story of a massacre continue to blossom? Professor Tauber replied: "The story of the massacre grew out of two elements: There was one case - which was reported by the Etzel, in which a group of Arabs left the house and surrendered, but an Etzel fighter shot at them with a machine gun. This is the only exception. This happened in the lower part of the village. When an event happens at the bottom, all the Arabs in the upper part of the village can see it and, indeed, everyone focuses on that one family in their reports. Later, a foreign journalist interviewed one of the family members who was wounded, and she talked about shots at a family."

Tauber continued: "Hussein al-Khalidi, the Supreme Secretary of the Arab Committee in Jerusalem, then the senior political figure in Jerusalem, was wondering how to enlist the Arab world in a struggle in which the local Arabs didn't have a chance [on their own]. He told his aide, Hassan Nusseibeh, that they must begin to engage in propaganda because they do not interest the Arab countries. 'We have to tell Deir Yassin, not as it really happened, but to exaggerate it,' he said.

"We know this from Hassan Nusseibeh himself, as he has said so in interviews. And then they started to say that 254 people were killed and raped, and the problem of rape is the one that scared the Palestinians more than the killings, giving the story worldwide circulation. As the Arabs say, the person who caused this catastrophe is Hussein al-Khalidi.

"In the book I say that he wanted to prevent a catastrophe, but ended up causing one. It may be that from the logical point of view he did the logical thing, but things went wrong and that [false story] was the number one factor in the flight of the Arabs from Israel. That is how the myth was created," said Tauber, who noted that Al-Khalidi's assistant was responsible for the Arab radio broadcast from Jerusalem, so that the exaggerated story that they decided to spread could be immediately broadcast without British censorship. "Within minutes, the story spread across Israel with all the significance [with which it had been purposely imbued]."

And how was the myth born from the Israeli angle, the angle of historians like Meir Pa'il and others? "People like Pa'il came only at four o'clock, an hour and a half after the battle ended, as he himself attests in a report he did not think would be revealed to the public, and as his photographer Shraga Peled, who arrived only an hour later, attests. Likewise with Yechezkel Rabi and Mordechai Gihon, who was the first to arrive and said that he arrived half an hour later. They arrived after the event, and the sights were indeed terrible. Lehi and Etzel members attempted to dispose of the corpses by burning them. The stench was awful."

Tauber also disproved the oft-cited claim that an Arab man was burned alive after being tied to a tree.

"They [who make this claim] do not know what happened in the village. The Arab was Abd Allah 'Abd al-Majid Samur, a fighter who tried to escape on the trucks carrying the women and children. At that point, they identified him and shot him and tied the corpse to a tree to burn it. "They did not burn an Arab alive."

On the interests that led to spreading the myth in the Jewish public, Professor Tauber explains: "Gihon, whose report should be read in its original form, included a remark that the operation attracted great sympathy for the dissidents and that propaganda needed to be produced to present the incident as a military and moral failure. Later these comments were omitted. Meir Pa'il came an hour and a half after the battle and related in his original report that he had seen corpses which he assumed had died in a massacre, meaning that he didn't see one, but only imagined what had happened.

"Because he stood at the head of the unit working against [the underground Zionist groups vying with the Palmach] Etzel and

Lehi, he described the incident as if he had seen the shooting with his own eyes and saw how they fired at people in the quarry. He claimed that there were photographs, but his photographer says he took pictures of dead bodies and not of the shooting itself. All the pictures are of dead bodies and not of the actual shooting."

Tauber also noted that the Arab stories about the battle of Deir Yassin later reached delusional levels, while abroad the story is presented in such a way as to turn the Jews into Nazis. Nevertheless, he mentioned a blunt quote from an Arab interviewee who was asked whether there had been rape incidents in the village. He responded that this claim was false. "And the interviewer, who understands the effect of this rumor, says 'In other words, the Jews are free of guilt on these matters, but we still have lost our lands.'"

The Palestinian-Israeli Conflict Is a Land Dispute

Cecil Maranville

In the following viewpoint, Cecil Maranville provides an overview of the long history of land dispute between Palestinians and Israelis. The conflict began in the forties, when Great Britain promised land to both Israelis and Palestinians, not realizing they would both want the same land. After the 1948 war between Israel and five Arab nations, the victorious Israelis took control of what is now known as Israel. Ownership of the land is a complex issue, as occupation of Palestine goes back to Biblical times. Maranville argues that based on the original covenant with God, the land belongs to everyone. Cecil Maranville is "a minister of the Church of God," working as a writer, editor, and speaker.

As you read, consider the following questions:

1. Why does the author claim that the Palestinian-Israeli conflict is a land dispute and not a religious one?
2. How did Great Britain's actions after World War II complicate the situation?
3. Why does Maranville claim, based on history, that the land belongs to everyone?

S ome claim that the Palestinians have been forced off their land and that they have been deprived of what is rightfully theirs.

"Palestine Israel Whose Land Is It, Really," by Cecil Maranville, United Church of God, June 4, 2002. Reprinted by permission.

Others maintain that the Israelis have a legitimate entitlement to their nation, including the lands seized in war action. The current US administration has begun to use the word "occupy" in reference to Israeli military presence in Palestinian towns, implying that the Israelis have invaded sovereign territory. Whose land is it, really? Frankly, the answer may surprise you.

"Palestine" is a term that essentially corresponds to a section of land in southwest Asia at the eastern end of the Mediterranean Sea. That same territory comprises the modern Israeli state. Since becoming a nation in 1948, the Israelis have developed a productive, fertile and wealthy nation in a desert wasteland. They have been outstanding custodians of their homeland.

But, is it their homeland? Or, is it the Palestinians' homeland? "Palestinians" is the commonly used appellation for the descendants of approximately 780,000 Arabs who were displaced by a war between five Arab nations and the newly proclaimed state of Israel in 1948.

When the war began, some of the Arabs abandoned their homes in fear, while others left believing that they would soon return. Of course, they did not anticipate that the Israelis would win the war, much less such a lopsided victory. Since that time, these displaced peoples and their descendants have lived in temporary camps without a land they could call their own.

The bitter dispute over the ownership of Palestine continues to this day. Neither people is willing to accept the other's claim to total control of the territory that both consider their own. As with any complex dispute, there are many ways of presenting the issues involved.

How the Israelis Came to Possess the Land

The Israelis believe that they have a legitimate claim for several reasons. Not the least of which is that they successfully defended it against overwhelming numbers in the late 1940s and subsequent wars. Is the land theirs, because they have been able to defend it? How did it come to be theirs in the first place?

Turning back the clock to the two and a half decades leading up to the establishment of the Israeli nation, the land of Palestine was under the control of the British. For political reasons, the British promised a Palestinian homeland both to resident Arabs and to Jewish immigrants. The Arabs had helped the British overthrow the Ottoman Turks and were promised control of their land in return for their allegiance. So, the Palestinian Arabs could rightly claim ownership of land in which many of them had lived. But, does that fact make it their land?

At the same time that the British gave the land to their Arab friends, they were also interested in currying the political support of Jews in different parts of the British Empire. So they promised the same land to the Jews! Therefore, both peoples could claim that the land had been given to them!

Failing to understand the passion in the heart of both peoples, the British did not anticipate that the Arab Palestinians and the Jews would want the same land.

When the British-Arab alliance freed Jerusalem from Ottoman rule in 1917, the Arab Palestinians vastly outnumbered Jewish settlers. That, in spite of the fact that from the 1880s, Jewish refugees had been pouring into the area. Due to an intensification of anti-Semitism, Theodor Herzl had founded the World Zionist Organization in 1897, proposing that European Jews immigrate to Palestine and have freedom from persecution.

Immigration increased dramatically in the 1930s, with Nazism at its peak, when world sympathy inclined towards the Jews. Even so, the British attempted to limit Jewish immigration to Palestine in deference to their Arab allies. It was in this climate that the British found themselves promising the land of Palestine to both Arabs and Jews.

Acts of terrorism in today's Palestine headline the news almost daily, as homicide bombers blow themselves up in public places in Israel, slaughtering and maiming innocent Israeli citizens. However, terrorism was practiced by both sides in those years of upheaval, before the 1947-48 Arab-Israeli war ended with Israel in control of most of Palestine. One Jewish terrorist who planned and carried out strikes against the occupying British troops later became a prime minister of Israel—Menachem Begin. He was famous for referring to the land of Palestine as "Judea" and "Samaria," names the land held when occupied by ancient Israel.

Unable to negotiate an acceptable settlement, the British turned to the United Nations to resolve the complex issue.

In 1947, the UN proposed what appeared to be a logical solution—partitioning the land between the two peoples. The mufti of Jerusalem, the spokesman for the Palestinian Arabs, rejected it. The Jewish immigrants, at the time, accepted the idea. Under the leadership of David Ben Gurion, Israel declared itself a state on May 14, 1948. In spite of superior numbers, the Palestinian Arabs fled from the Israelis, counting on their Arab brothers to crush the upstart nation and return Palestine to their control.

Of course, that didn't happen.

Who Had It First Doesn't Solve the Dilemma

If we attempt to settle the Palestinian question by the concept of "who was there first," we meet with obvious difficulties. If we go back to the late 19th century and the early 20th century, the Arabs were in Palestine first. So, is the land rightfully theirs? Not so fast. Let's go back further—thousands of years further.

Historians believe the first major population to inhabit the land was the Canaanites. If "possession is 9/10ths of the law," the land belonged to them and their descendants. But, a militarily powerful people known as Philistines migrated into the Canaanite land, and it's their name that is thought to have evolved into "Palestine." So, is it their descendants who can rightfully claim the land of Palestine is theirs?

It's not that simple, either.

Another people migrated into the land of Canaan—they were the descendants of a man named "Eber," whose name meant "the other side." They were known as "Hebrews," coming from "the other side" of the Euphrates into Canaan. Their most famous patriarch was Abraham.

Genesis 12 records his immigration to Canaan. When he and his family arrived in the territory, an amazing event happened. The Creator God appeared to Abram, as he was known at the time, and made a remarkable promise: "To your descendants I will give this land" (verse 7). You can't get higher authority than that—greater than the militant Philistines, superior to the grand British Empire, senior to the United Nations—the Supreme God gave the land away. Possession wasn't the determining factor of right to ownership; the Canaanites had it taken out from under them.

Since the Jews are Abraham's children, the land is theirs after all. Right? No, it's still not that simple. Two vast peoples descended from Abraham's two sons, Isaac and Ishmael. From Isaac came Jacob, also named Israel and from him 12 clans (or 13, depending on how they are configured). The Jews are the descendants of only one of those tribes, that of Judah.

Further, the descendants of Ishmael are the Arabs! So, who has the right to the land of Palestine?

God's promise to Abraham was repeated to Isaac and then to Jacob (Israel), making clear that His intent was that Isaac's line would be the one to inherit the land.

Jews and Muslims Lay a Religious Claim to the Land

History was neither soft nor kind to Israel, for it had to fight to occupy and hold the land. Civil war divided the country into two nations, known as Judea and Samaria. It was to this rough and tumble period of Palestine's history that Menachem Begin referred by calling modern Palestine by those names. He meant to emphasize that the Jews had a religious claim to the land.

Religion is also a factor in the Palestinian view. According to the CIA's World Factbook, the religious preference of 75 percent of the Palestinians is Muslim. Beginning in the seventh century, Muslims began a 1,300-year reign over what was initially known as

---

A Conflict over Territory

The Palestinian-Israeli conflict is, in essence, a conflict over territory. It began as a struggle over the control of the land of Palestine between the native Palestinian Arab population and Zionism, a European political movement aiming to establish a Jewish state. Realization of the Zionist dream necessarily involved displacement and dispossession of the Palestinian Arabs who lived there and owned most of the land.

The Zionist goals were accomplished both during cataclysmic events such as the wars of 1948 and 1967, and through other more subtle, systematic, legal, and political means, leaving the Palestinians no choice but to struggle for national self-determination in their historical homeland.

Although religion plays a role in defining the identities of the parties to the conflict, and for some Jews, in justifying their claims to the land, the conflict is not, fundamentally, a religious conflict. Early leaders of the Zionist movement were not particularly religious, just as many Israelis today are secular in outlook.

Recently, Islamic organizations such as Hamas have gained political power among Palestinians, lending the conflict a more religious hue than in the past. Nonetheless, a variety of indices suggests that Hamas has gained power less from devotion to its ultimate aim of creating an Islamic state in all of Palestine than from the failures of the secular nationalist Palestine Liberation Organization (PLO) leadership.

"What Is the Palestinian-Israeli Conflict Really About?" Institute for Middle East Understanding, November 7, 2005.

"Filastin," a precursor to "Palestine." (A connection to the ancient Philistines is obvious.)

"Palestine was holy to Muslims because the Prophet Muhammad had designated Jerusalem as the first qibla (the directions Muslims face when praying) and because he was believed to have ascended on a night journey to heaven from the area of Solomon's temple, where the Dome of the Rock was later built. Jerusalem became the third holiest city of Islam" (Encarta Online Encyclopedia, 2002, "Palestine," p. 4).

Professor Moshe Sharon, who has a doctorate in medieval Islamic history from Hebrew University in Jerusalem, lectured last fall on "The Agenda of Islam." Dr. Sharon addressed the correlation between "Islam and Territory," according to the strictest school of Islamic law: "This civilization created one very important, fundamental rule about territory. Any territory that comes under Islamic rule cannot be de-Islamized. Even if at one time or another, the [non-Muslim] enemy takes over the territory that was under Islamic rule, it is considered to be perpetually Islamic. This is why whenever you hear about the Arab/Israeli conflict, you hear: territory, territory, territory. There are other aspects to the conflict, but territory is highly important" (www.mjaa.org).

Therefore, many Palestinian Muslims believe they also have a religious claim to the land of Palestine. That is why they have fought and will continue to fight so ferociously for it.

The intensity of the passion on both sides of this complex issue is no less than it was in 1947, when both the Arabs and Jews believed that they had a right—the full right of ownership—to Palestine.

So, whose land is it? Remember, one no less than the Creator God claimed ownership of the land and the right to name its inheritor. To whom did He give it?

The Land Goes to the Covenant People

From the beginning of the promises He made to Abraham, and then repeated to Isaac, Israel and his children, God intertwined those promises in a pact called a covenant. It was not the type of covenant which is negotiated between equals, but rather the type of agreement that is imposed by a suzerain or sovereign on a people that he has conquered. In essence, God told these people He chose for a unique purpose: "For My part, I promise to give you the land of Canaan [Palestine]. For your part, you will live by the regulations or the holy law that I give you. If you break your part of the covenant, I'm no longer bound by My Word."

Psalm 105 is but one of numerous references to this covenant, which named the land of Palestine as part of the divinely bequeathed benefits: "O seed of Abraham His servant, you children of Jacob, His chosen ones! He is the Lord our God; His judgments are in all the earth. He remembers His covenant forever, the word which He commanded, for a thousand generations, the covenant which He made with Abraham, and His oath to Isaac, and confirmed it to Jacob for a statute, to Israel as an everlasting covenant, saying, 'To you I will give the land of Canaan as the allotment of your inheritance'" (verses 6-11).

But, the people were expected to "observe His statutes and keep His laws" (verse 45).

With the passage of time, they drifted from their obligations. Generous and gracious, God worked with them for much longer than He was obligated to do. Yet the time came when He finally declared that the covenant was broken: "The earth is also defiled under its inhabitants, because they have transgressed the laws, changed the ordinance, broken the everlasting covenant" (Isaiah 24:5).

So which descendants of Abraham have a right to the land of Palestine? The ones to whom God initially gave it broke the deal and have no more claim to the land than any other ethnic group, if we look to the One who has the sole right to give it away.

Has Abraham no descendants, then, who are "covenant people," whose right of inheritance is this much-bloodied land? Ah, but he does! God actually expanded the land promise to include the entire earth (Romans 4:13), and those who are part of God's New Covenant will be co-inheritors of it. For more information about this remarkable truth, see our booklet The Gospel of the Kingdom.

Periodical and Internet Sources Bibliography

The following articles have been selected to supplement the diverse views presented in this chapter.

Ramzy Baroud, "What Is Next for Palestine?" *Aljazeera,* January 18, 2018. https://www.aljazeera.com/indepth/opinion /palestine-180116110352197.html.

Roger Cohen, "Israel-Palestine from Both Sides of the Mirror," *New York Times,* June 16, 2017. https://www.nytimes.com/2017/06/16 /opinion/israel-palestine-from-both-sides-of-the-mirror.html.

Guardian, "The *Guardian* View on Israel and Palestine: Escape the Past," *Guardian,* November 2, 2017. https://www.theguardian .com/commentisfree/2017/nov/01/the-guardian-view-on-israel -and-palestine-escape-the-past.

David Harris, "Ten Basic Facts About the Israeli-Palestinian Conflict," *Huffington Post,* December 25, 2017. https://www.huffingtonpost .com/entry/ten-basic-facts-about-the-israeli-palestinian-conflict_ us_5a417601e4b0df0de8b066a2.

Yara Hawari, "The Spectacle of Palestine," *Aljazeera,* December 10, 2017. https://www.aljazeera.com/indepth/opinion/spectacle -palestine-171210104249089.html.

History of the Israeli-Palestinian Conflict, *Pro-con.org,* July 22, 2015. https://israelipalestinian.procon.org/view.timeline .php?timelineID=000031.

Jewish Voice for Peace, "Israel Palestine Conflict 101." https:// jewishvoiceforpeace.org/israeli-palestinian-conflict-101.

Efraim Karsh, "1948, Israel, and the Palestinians—The True Story," *Commentary,* May 1, 2008. https://www.commentarymagazine .com/articles/1948-israel-and-the-palestinians-the-true-story.

Mark N. Katz, "The Israeli-Palestinian Conflict and the War on Terror," *Middle East Policy Council.* http://www.mepc.org /commentary/israeli-palestinian-conflict-and-war-terror.

GLOBALVIEWPOINTS

CHAPTER 2

Is the BDS Movement Justified and Effective?

The BDS Movement Is Justified and Cannot Be Stopped

Miko Peled

The US Congress has voted to outlaw the Palestinian BDS movement in the United States. In the following viewpoint Miko Peled, an Israeli, argues staunchly against this law. Peled, who comes from a prominent Israeli family and is a Jewish defender of the BDS movement, believes that Israel's treatment of the Palestinians has been unjust and that many Israelis agree with him, including high ranking members of the military. Though US Senator Chuck Shumer has called BDS a form of anti-Semitism, Peled believes that the BDS movement does not hurt or kill individual Jews but merely demands that Palestinians are given equal rights in Israel, including the right of refugees to return to their native land. Peled is an Israeli human rights activist who lives in Washington DC. He is the author of The General's Son, Journey of an Israeli in Palestine *and the forthcoming book* Injustice, The Story of the Holy Land Foundation Five.

As you read, consider the following questions:

1. Why has the US Congress come out against the BDS movement?
2. Why is Miko Peled a particularly strong voice for the Palestinian movement?
3. What are the arguments for and against the BDS movement being anti-Semitic in this viewpoint?

"The BDS Movement Is Justified and Cannot Be Stopped," by MIko Peled, PopularResistance.Org, August 1, 2017. Reprinted by permission.

Note: In order to protect Israel, Members of Congress are currently trying to outlaw the constitutional right to freedom of speech and the political right to organize a boycott. Margaret Flowers and Kevin Zeese interview Miko Peled, author of *The General's Son*.

Peled grew up in Israel in a family that could be called Israeli royalty: his ancestors were fighting for a Jewish State decades before Israel was created. His grandfather signed the Declaration of Independence, a founding document of Israel. His father became a soldier in the war for independence, the 1948 Arab-Israeli war, and he was a general in the Arab-Israeli war of 1967. Peled began a military career as a Red Beret in the Israeli Defense Forces but today he is an advocate for Palestinian rights and a critic of Israel.

In our interview, he explodes myths we commonly hear about Israel. Peled explains that Israel is an apartheid state and not really a true democracy. He provides facts that explain the reality of segregation in Israel and what the lives of Palestinians are like in Israel and in the Palestinian territories. He also describes what moved him to reject his upbringing and what he had been taught in order to fight for Palestinian rights and support the BDS movement.

We ask him if it is fair to describe what is happening in Palestine as ethnic cleansing or genocide. Is Israel committing war crimes? And, what is the path to resolving this conflict for the betterment of the Palestinians and Israelis? And, we discuss how the true narrative of history raises questions about whether Israel is a legitimate nation.

For over a decade now, hundreds of Palestinian organizations have been calling for the world to impose boycotts, divestment and sanctions targeting illegal Israeli settlements, much as people boycotted South Africa during apartheid. The BDS movement, as it is known, has been an effective tool causing Israel to fight back. For years, state legislatures have introduced legislation to prevent participation in BDS. Now, led by Senator Ben Cardin, a similar but much more severe law has been introduced in Congress. Peled writes about that bill and why it must be stopped below.

The Senate BDS Bill: Repressing Freedom Of Speech Is Undemocratic

Repressing free speech is undemocratic, that was established in the First Amendment a long time ago, and the right to boycott is enshrined within that amendment, including the right to boycott Israeli products. It was also established long ago that all men and women, including Palestinians, are created equal and are deserving of the same rights to life liberty and the pursuit of happiness.

For many decades now, Jews around the world, including staunch Zionist Jews like the late Dr. Nahum Goldman and Professor Yishayahu Leibovitch had opposed the Israeli occupation of the West Bank and building Jewish settlements there – as have Israeli generals, former Mossad chiefs and countless lesser known Jewish people. But over the last fifty years consecutive Israeli governments of all parties have built Jewish settlements in the West Bank and no amount of talking and negotiating has made the slightest difference.

Israel claims that it has a small Arab minority sometimes called "The Arabs of Israel" and that they enjoy full citizenship rights. However, these are Palestinian Arabs and although they hold Israeli citizenship they do not enjoy the same rights as Israeli Jewish citizens. They live in separate cities and separate communities, go to different schools are given far less opportunities and poverty levels are considerably higher among them. From laws that limit who they may marry and where they may live to laws that limit their right to commemorate the "Naqba," the catastrophe that befell Palestinians when Israel was established, Palestinian citizens of Israel face discrimination at every stage of their lives, and still Israeli law makers continue to pass laws that discriminate against them at an alarming speed.

The Right of Return of Palestinians who were displaced in 1948 has been enshrined in article 11 of UN resolution 194. Furthermore, according to a report by the UN Economic and Social Commission for Western Asia the Law of Return, "conferring on Jews worldwide the right to enter Israel and obtain Israeli

NCCOP

The Palestinian National Committee for Boycott, Divestment and Sanctions (BNC) has warmly welcomed a historic open letter by the National Coalition of Christian Organizations in Palestine (NCCOP) urging the World Council of Churches (WCC) to "recognize Israel as an apartheid state," support the nonviolent, Palestinian-led global BDS movement, help intensify BDS campaigns and actively refuse Christian complicity in ongoing Israeli violations of Palestinian human rights.

Notably, the NCCOP recalled the WCC's "courageous and pivotal prophetic leadership" in its work to end the apartheid regime's racist rule in South Africa, and called on it to be consistent and play the same inspiring role in ending Israeli apartheid against the entire Palestinian people today.

Calling on the WCC to work against Christian complicity in sustaining Israeli apartheid, the NCCOP said it was "disturbed by the fact that States and churches are dealing with Israel as if the situation were normal, ignoring the reality of occupation, discrimination and daily death in the land."

The NCCOP specifically called on the World Council of Churches to defend the Palestinian right to advocate for BDS campaigns until Israel "complies with international law" and ends its regime of "occupation, apartheid and discriminations, and accepts [the right of] refugees to return to their home land and properties." In point 7 of its call to action, the NCCOP went further and asked the WCC to itself help "intensify" BDS measures.

The NCCOP represents a cross-section of the most prominent Christian Palestinian organizations in present-day Israel and the Occupied Palestinian Territory, including those in Jerusalem, Bethlehem, and Gaza. About 200,000 Christian Palestinians currently reside in historic Palestine, descendants of some of the oldest Christian communities in the world. As an integral part of the Palestinian people subjected to half a century of Israeli military occupation and nearly 70 years of ongoing dispossession and apartheid, they suffer from widespread official and unofficial Israeli discrimination and hate crimes, whether they are citizens of Israel, live under Israeli military rule or have been rendered refugees denied their right of return to their homeland.

"BNC Welcomes Call by Christian Organizations Urging the World Council of Churches to Support the BDS Movement for Palestinian Human Rights," IMEMC, June 20, 2017.

citizenship regardless of their countries of origin and whether or not they can show links to Israel-Palestine, while withholding any comparable right from Palestinians, including those with documented ancestral homes in the country." This was correctly referred to as a policy of "demographic engineering meant to uphold Israel's status as the Jewish state."

BDS have arguably become the three most controversial letters in the alphabet. Representing the call by Palestinian civil society to impose boycott, to divest and to impose sanctions on the State of Israel and companies that profit from the Israeli occupation. This call seeks to remedy the three conditions described above without harming or depriving anyone of their rights. BDS is controversial mostly because the call has been widely misrepresented. But the demands of the BDS movement neither express or intend any racism or violence towards anyone, they are as follows:

1. Ending the occupation.
2. Equal rights to all Palestinians.
3. Return of the Palestinian refugees.

According to a letter submitted by the ACLU to members of the US Senate, "S. 720 Israel Anti-Boycott Act is a bill that seeks to criminalize the call for BDS." It states that it "would punish businesses and individuals based solely on their political point of view" and "Such a penalty is in direct violation of the First Amendment." The letter ends by urging senators to oppose the bill.

In a speech made by Senator Chuck Schumer, one of the co-sponsors of this bill, regarding BDS at the American Jewish Committee's Global Forum on June 5, 2017, the Senator from New York said, "There is no greater example than this insidious effort to harm the Jewish state than through the boycotts, divestment and sanctions." However, in reading the demands of the BDS call, it is clear that its goals are to improve the conditions which Israel has imposed on Palestinians and to repair inequities which Israeli governments are unwilling to address. There is no question that all efforts to get Israel to repair the inequities without pressure, had been exhausted.

Schumer refers to BDS as "a modern form of anti-Semitism." Indeed, a modern form which does not incite against Jews, does not call for the killing of or discrimination against Jews but instead demands that all people who reside in Palestine/Israel enjoy the same rights and privileges.

Israel's Economic Strength Hinders the Effectiveness of BDS

Shir Hever

In the following excerpted viewpoint, Shir Hever argues that Israel's strong economy—it is the world's leading exporter of products such as fertilizer and also is a major player in the world arms trade—works against the BDS movement. Israel has also moved from decades of borrowing money to become a lender nation. These factors suggest that attempting to boycott Israeli goods may not be a successful strategy, especially because only a minuscule percentage of economic sanctions have their intended effect. The South African boycott that BDS is most often compared to were not particularly effective. Hever is an economic researcher in the Alternative Information Center, a Palestinian-Israeli organization active in Jerusalem and Beit-Sahour. He is the author of Political Economy of Israel's Occupation: Repression Beyond Exploitation.

As you read, consider the following questions:

1. What are the factors contributing to Israel's economic strength?
2. How has Israel used the US war on terror to its advantage?
3. How did past Arab boycotts of Israel fare?

[…]

"The Question of Sanctions and a Boycott Against Israel," by Shir Hever, Alternative Information Center, March 2006. Reprinted by permission.

S anctions are not always successful at achieving political results. Robert Pape, a professor of political science, claims that only 5% of economic sanctions are effective.[19]

The sanctions on South Africa, for example, are generally considered to have been ineffective, and to have played only a minor role in the abolition of the Apartheid regime there. South Africa's wealth of natural resources provided the government with an ample sup- ply of alternative raw materials, and its economy was thus able to withstand the pressures.[20]

Israel has a strong economy, and is a large exporter. It is the world's big- gest exporter of fertilizers, polished diamonds and industrial oils. It exports 57% of the total world exports of fertilizers, 34% of the total exports of polished diamonds, 26% of the total ex- ports of industrial oils and 12% of the total weapons sales.[21]

The question therefore arises, would sanctions put effective pressure on Israel at all?

Foreign Currency Surplus

Israel's international trade position is currently quite strong. After decades of borrowing money and dependency on foreign aid, in 2002 Israel became a lending market and has since remained one. The accumulated foreign aid that Israel received from the US and Germany gave Israel a powerful base of foreign currency which strengthened its economy.[22]

In 2005, Israel lent over US $20.8 billion to countries and companies around the world. Most of the loans were given by private banks and other financial businesses.[23]

One indication of Israel's strengthening position in the global economy is the increase in the reserves held by the Central Bank of Israel (CBI); these have seen a marked rise since 1996. In 2005, the governor of the CBI stated that he believes that the Israeli market is very strong, as demonstrated by the exchange.[24]

Another factor is Israel's dependence on exports. If Israel was forced to rely only on the reserves held by the CBI (without revenue from exports), it could continue importing only for a limited time. One indication of Israel's ability to withstand sanctions is the length of time over which the CBI reserves could fund imports. This is a tradeoff between the size of the CBI reserves, and the lev- el of imports that Israel has become accustomed to.

Over the years, the number of days for which the CBI could support imports has increased. The major factor contributing to this increase was a 1996 U.S grant of US $9 billion.

As a result, in 1998 Israel had the highest effective reserves ever—enough for 194 days of imports. Since then the reserves are gradually eroding again.[25]

Another contribution to the flow of foreign currency into Israel was the increased humanitarian assistance to the OPT. Starting in 1994, international donors began funneling humanitarian assistance to the Palestinians in an effort to stave off the humanitarian crisis in the OPT. Israel imposes a series of taxes and tariffs on this aid, which, along with outright confiscations, allow it to appropriate large portions of these funds.[26]

The increase in effective reserves took place despite the fact that the total expenditure on imports has increased. [It] demonstrates that exports are gradually catching up to imports, and that Israel's trade deficit is therefore on the decline.[27]

According to Israel's Central Bureau of Statistics, exports sharply increased in 2004, a further indication of Israel's strong position in the world market. While this data is reported to be grossly exaggerated, there are new indications that in 2005 exports continue to in- crease, especially exports to Europe.[28]

The Arms Trade

Israel is one of the biggest arms producers, importers and exporters in the world. In 2001, Israel was the 10th biggest arms exporter in the world, and was able to export 75% of its total arms pro- duction (the remainder was for domes- tic use). That year, Israel provided 10% of the total arms exports in the world. In the past decade, Israel sold various military systems to over 57 countries.[29]

In arms sales to developing countries, however, Israel is the 4th biggest seller. In 2004, Israel's sale of armaments to developing countries amounted to US $1.2 billion, falling below only the US, Russia and the UK.[30]

Israel's exports improved after September 11, as Israel pursued a foreign policy which conflates its suppression of the Palestinian resistance with the US "War on Terrorism." This foreign policy had some success, as Israeli military companies reinforced their reputation as "experts" in fighting terrorism and substantially increased their export profits.[31]

The Arab Boycott

The Arab Boycott on Israel constituted the first and most well-known sanctions against Israel: its apparent failure suggests that future sanctions may also fail.

Arab countries have boycotted Israel even before the state was officially declared. The boycott was initiated to protest the overtaking of Palestinian lands by the Zionist movement, which the Arab nations perceived as yet another colonial movement. Once the state was declared, the boycott prohibited direct trade with Israel and was also directed at companies that traded with Israel.[32]

During the first decades of Israel's existence and up to the late 80s and early 90s, the effects of this boycott on Israel were relatively marginal. Firstly, the world was less globalized then, and Israel was content to maintain trade relations with a limited number of nations. Secondly, at the time national ideals were far more important to most Israelis than any remote prospects of attaining wealth through international trade. Austerity was viewed as a patriotic sacrifice, and the Israeli economy was still centered on agriculture and industry, rather than on trade.[33]

In 1977, the US Congress passed a bill prohibiting US companies from co-operating with the Arab boycott. Many other countries joined the US opposition to the boycott.[34]

Since 1993 and the dawn of the Oslo peace process, the boycott was gradually eliminated as many countries stopped abiding by it. In July 2001, several Arab countries attempted to reinstate the boycott in response to the massive Israeli attacks against the Palestinian population during the second Intifada, but this attempt met with little success.[35]

The final blow to the Arab Boycott seems imminent. As Saudi Arabia prepares to join the World Bank Organization (WTO), it is required to lift sanctions from Israel. Thus one of the countries which implemented the Arab Boycott on Israel most strictly will withdraw it. Under US pressure, Persian Gulf countries have also announced that they will withdraw the boycott.[36] Israeli economists estimate that between 1950 and 1993 the boycott cost the Israeli economy no more than US \$45-\$49 billion.[37]

The failure of the Arab boycott raises important questions. Are boycott attempts against Israel destined to fail? Will the WHO serve to defend Israel from sanctions?

[…]

Notes

(19) Pape, Robert, 1997, "Why Economic Sanc- tions Do Not Work?," *International Security*, Vol. 22, no. 2, Fall 1997, p. 90-136.

(20) Levy, Philip L., 1999, *Sanctions on South Africa: What Did They Do?*, Economic Growth Center, Yale University, Discussion Paper No. 796, February 1999, p. 2-14.

(21) Ynet, 2005, "Israel Rose to the 8th Place in Per Capita World Exports," *Ynet*, 8.11.05. See also Bar- zilai, Amnon, 2004, "The Rebels and I," *Haaretz*, 15.9.04.

(22) Israeli Central Bureau of Statistics, various years, http://www1.cbs.gov.il/reader/shnaton/ text_search_heb_new.html?CYear=2005&Vol=5 6&input=%e4%fa%e7%e9%e9%e1%e5%e9%e5%fa+%ec%e7%e5%f5+%ec%e0%f8%f5. About for- eign aid to Israel, see Hever, Shir, 2005, *Foreign Aid to the Occupied Palestinian Territories and Israel*, The Alternative Information Center, June 2005.

(23) Klein, Zeev, 2005, "Israel's External Debt in the First Half of 2005 Was US \$73.9 Billion – A Reduction of 0.5%," *Globes*, 7-8.9.05.

(24) Globes, 2005, "Fischer: "The Exchange Rate is Great for Us; The Power of the Market Stems from the Russian Immigration," *Globes*, 14-15.9.05.

(25) ICBS, various years, and Zuriel-Harari, Keren, 2005, "Plan Growth Regardless of the Disengage- ment," *Globes*, 14-15.8.05.

(26) Deen, Thalif, 2002, "Israel Taxes Humanitar- ian Aid to Palestinians - U.N.," *Common Dreams News Center, 26.9.05,* and Hever, Shir, 2005, *For- eign Aid to the OPT and Israel.*

(27) ICBS, various years.

(28) Koren, Ora, 2004, "Exporters: Essential Turn n Exports in 2004; Will Reach US \$21.4 Billion," *Haaretz*, 4.5.04, Koren, Orna, 2004, "Embarrass- ment in the CBI: Con icting Data on Exports In- crease in First Quarter of 2004," *Haaretz*, 19.5.04, and

Manor, Hadas, 2005, "Exports to the Euro- pean Union Increased by 11% at the Half Year," *Globes*, 14-15.8.05.

(29) Turner, Mandy, 2002, *Arming the Occupa- tion: Israel and the Arms Trade*, CAAT Report, http://www.caat.org.uk/information/publica- tions/countries/israel-1002.php and Barzilai, Am- non, 2004, "The Rebels and I," *Haaretz*, 15.9.04.

(30) Amit, Eitan, 2005, "Israel – The Biggest Weapons Exporter in the World in 2004," *Globes*, 31.8.05-1.9.05.

(31) Barzilai, Amnon, 2004, "The Exports Insti- tute: Security Companies Will Export US $4 Billion By the End of the Decade," *Haaretz*, 30.1.04, and Turner, Mandy, 2002, *Arming the Occupation: Israel and the Arms Trade*, CAAT Report, http:// www.caat. org.uk/information/publications/coun- tries/israel-1002.php.

(32) Solidarity With Israel, *Timeline of Modern Israeli History 1924-1964*, http://www. solidarity- withisrael.org/history/part2.cfm.

(33) Filk, Dani, 2004, "Israel Model 2000: Neo- Liberal Post-Fordism," in Ram, Uri and Filk, Dani (eds), *The Power of Property: Israeli Society in the Global Age*, Van-Leer Institute, Jerusalem, p. 16-33; and Shalev, Michael, 2004, "Did Globaliza- tion and Liberalization 'Normalize' Israeli Political Economy?," ibid, p. 84-115.

(34) Solidarity With Israel, *Timeline of Modern Israeli History 1924-1964*.

(35) Ibid.

(36) Hasi, Elyahu, 2005, "Saudi Arabia Is on Its Way to Join the Trade Organization; The Boycott on Israel Will Be Eased," *Globes*, 11-12.9.05, and Perri, Smadar, 2005, "Gulf- Principalities: We Will Withdraw the Economic Boycott on Israel," *Globes*, 25-26.9.05.

(37) Gillerman, Danny, 1993, p. 18-19.

The Implications of Academic BDS Are Complicated

Ingrid Matthews and James Arvanitakis

In the following viewpoint, Ingrid Matthews and James Arvanitakis debate the concept of academic BDS. The authors argue that debates about BDS gets sidetracked with accusations of anti-Semitism rather than human rights issues. They outright reject anti-Semitism. Instead, they examine the effectiveness of academic boycott, the refusal to support Israeli education institutions that participate in or benefit from Israel's occupation of the West Bank. The authors explain that the case for academic BDS hinges on academic integrity and freedom, while the case against academic BDS lies in highlighting other forms of activism instead. Matthews is a masters research student at the Centre for Peace and Conflict Studies at the University of Sydney, investigating western media coverage of Israel and Palestine. Arvanitakis is Professor in Cultural and Social Analysis at Western Sydney University.

As you read, consider the following questions:

1. What is academic BDS?
2. Why is it important for the authors to state that academic BDS operates at the institutional level?
3. What is the "double harm argument" according to the viewpoint?

"Israel and the BDS Debate: Two Academics Respectfully Agree to Differ," by Ingrid Matthews and James Arvanitakis, The Conversation, August 20, 2015. https://theconversation.com/israel-and-the-bds-debate-two-academics-respectfully-agree-to-differ-44708 Licensed under a CC BY-ND 4.0.

From Australia, we watch Israel at a great distance, safe in the knowledge that the regular and horrific levels of violence in the region are far from our shores. But we still find ourselves, like most of the world, asking: what can we do? One response is the Boycott, Divestment and Sanctions (BDS) movement, which protests against documented human rights abuses perpetrated by Israel, such as settlement expansion on Palestinian land.

The purpose of economic BDS is to put pressure on nation states that are consistently in breach of international law and the principles enunciated in the Universal Declaration of Human Rights.

The Implications of Academic BDS

Our focus here is the implications of academic BDS. This is the call to academia to disengage from Israeli education institutions that endorse, participate in or benefit from the Israeli occupation of the West Bank and East Jerusalem, illegal settlement expansion and the blockade of Gaza.

We are colleagues who share many views and identify ourselves as academic-activists. Our pedagogy is shaped by social justice principles. But, when it comes to academic boycott, we hold different positions, which are more complex than simply withdrawing custom from Israeli businesses.

One of us has chosen to support academic BDS. That support is founded on the democratic principle that academic BDS is a people's movement of legitimate non-violent alternatives, because international and state institutions have failed to hold Israel to account.

The other rejects the academic boycott, but stresses that individuals and organisations have the right to support academic boycott without being professionally pressured or accused of anti-Semitism.

It should go without saying that BDS specifically rejects anti-Semitism in any form. Academic BDS operates at the institutional level—it is not about condemning individuals for their Jewish identity.

Academic Integrity and Freedom

The best of intellectual traditions seek co-operation and dialogue, in a free flow of ideas, to find solutions to intractable problems. To the principles of academic integrity and freedom, we add awareness-raising as integral to teaching.

This includes standing against abuse, apathy and inaction. As the then Australian Chief of Army, Lieutenant General David Morrison, famously said of sexism and sexual assault in the armed forces:

> The standard you walk past is the standard you accept.

The Double Harm Argument

The case against academic BDS questions whether it derails effective alternative activism. This is explored by Noam Chomsky, who eschews the centring of academic freedom (and themselves) by BDS proponents:

> Failed initiatives harm the victims doubly – by shifting attention from their plight to irrelevant issues (anti-Semitism at Harvard, academic freedom etc) and by wasting current opportunities to do something meaningful.

While BDS potentially ignores constructive Israeli voices, the more destructive voices build up their platform in the breach. When the Israeli Defence Force bombed United Nations buildings in Gaza, The Australian reported that Zionist law firm Shurat HaDin warned that academics who supported BDS would be "next in the firing line" for a lawsuit.

This became their story, when Israel was bombing international humanitarian infrastructure.

The question here is whether we compromise one form of solidarity for another. The findings of Israeli academics who work for human rights, who document the conflict and who theorise resolution cannot be devoid of all merit. We cannot incorporate their conclusions if we opt against working together.

A Risk of Losing Sight of the Key Concerns

All too often, the debate is lost in a cacophony of anti-Semitism accusations and the focus shifts to Western institutions instead of Palestinian rights. Our answer is neither to shout back, nor to go quietly into the relatively gentle Australian night.

BDS, and resistance to it, are founded in passionate commitment. As academics, we must locate reason in the actions, the words and the many complex human transactions that make up a campaign and a bilateral friendship.

Whether we support BDS and commit to promoting it, or decide to support the rights of those who do so, we are making a moral and ethical decision that is integral to our practice.

Like It or Not, Artists Who Perform in Israel Are Aligning Themselves with an Oppressive Regime

Ran Greenstein

In the following viewpoint Ran Greenstein argues that entertainers and athletes who perform in Israel are supporting Israel's actions against the Palestinian people, whether they consider themselves political actors or not. The author uses the example of South African DJ Black Coffee's concert in Israel and the resulting criticism against him to examine the importance and effectiveness of boycotting, noting that the artist was especially criticized because of his own country's history with apartheid. But refusing to play in Israel is not the only way to fight its regime, he maintains. It is also important to actively support progressive artists and initiatives within the country. Greenstein is an Associate Professor in the Department of Sociology at the University of the Witwatersrand Johannesburg, South Africa.

"Why South Africa's DJ Black Coffee left a bitter taste by performing in Israel," by Ran Greenstein, The Conversation, April 22, 2018. https://theconversation.com/why-south-africas-dj-black-coffee-left-a-bitter-taste-by-performing-in-israel-95311 Licensed under CC BY-ND 4.0.

As you read, consider the following questions:

1. Why is it significant that the artist in question is South African?
2. According to the author, what is a common defense against the argument that artists who defy the boycott are aligning with Israel?
3. What percentage of the Palestinian population have Israeli citizenship according to the viewpoint?

I t was a coincidence that South African house DJ Black Coffee's recent performance in Tel Aviv took place on the same weekend that saw more than a dozen Palestinian protesters shot dead, and more than a thousand wounded, by Israeli forces. But he was nevertheless criticised sharply for the visit which came in the wake of calls by political movements and civil society organisations to respect the boycott campaign against Israel.

Criticism was levelled against him from a number of fronts. This included South Africa's ruling African National Congress (ANC) which issued a call on artists to remember the role played by the international anti-apartheid solidarity movement in the isolation of apartheid South Africa:

> The people of Palestine are in a just cause for self determination and we urge our artists not to form part of the normalisation of Israeli's suppression of the Palestinian people in their quest for self determination and statehood that mirrors our very own struggle.

In response, the artist asserted his right to work as an entertainer and feed his family.

> Like everyone else I have rights and free will and no Black Coffee is not a political party...I work as an entertainer to feed my Family. To sum it up ... I'll take a bullet for my Family.

Born Nkosinathi Innocent Maphumulo, the hugely popular, multiaward winning Black Coffee is seen as the flag-bearer of South

Tom Yorke's Response to Criticisms Against Radiohead

After dozens of high-profile artists signed a letter in February urging Radiohead to cancel their upcoming concert in Tel Aviv, some might have assumed that the band would not respond to the criticism. After all, the British band's lead singer, Thom Yorke, rarely gives interviews, and the Israeli-Palestinian conflict is a particularly fraught issue to comment upon.

But oh, has Yorke responded.

In an interview with Rolling Stone's Andy Greene published on Friday, Yorke fired back at his critics for assuming that the members of Radiohead are uninformed on the Israeli-Palestinian issue. He argued that the authors of the letter — which rehashes the principle ideas driving the Boycott, Divestment and Sanctions movement against Israel, which aims to to exert economic and political pressure on Israel due to its policies toward Palestinians — waste their energy by throwing the word "apartheid" around....

There are people I admire [who have been critical of the concert] like [English film director] Ken Loach, who I would never dream of telling where to work or what to do or think. The kind of dialogue that they want to engage in is one that's black or white. I have a problem with that. It's deeply distressing that they choose to, rather than engage with us personally, throw shit at us in public. It's deeply disrespectful to assume that we're either being misinformed or that we're so retarded we can't make these decisions ourselves. I thought it was patronizing in the extreme. It's offensive and I just can't understand why going to play a rock show or going to lecture at a university [is a problem to them].

Yorke also pointed out that Radiohead guitarist Jonny Greenwood is married to an Arab-Israeli woman — and is subsequently uniquely informed about the nuances of the Israeli-Palestinian conflict.

The person who knows most about these things is Jonny [Greenwood]. He has both Palestinian and Israeli fans and a wife who's an Arab-Israeli. All these people to stand there at a distance throwing stuff at us, waving flags, saying, 'You don't know anything about it!' Imagine how offensive that is for Jonny. And imagine how upsetting that it's been to have this out there. Just to assume that we know nothing about this...

"Thom Yorke Calls Critics of Radiohead's Israel Concert 'Offensive,'" by Gabe Friedman,
Jewish Telegraphic Agency, June 2, 2017.

African Afro-house music. In 2015 he won the "Breakthrough DJ Of The Year" award in Ibiza and the next year he became the first South African to win a BET award in the "best international act Africa" category.

Accolades like these, and many others, paved the way to international stardom with major DJ gigs and even more album sales. Because of this rising global profile, his decision to play in Israel caused a major stir.

The Case for the Boycott

Cases like Black Coffee's aren't rare. Many internationally renowned artists have faced campaigns to convince them not to perform in Israel in solidarity with the Palestinian liberation struggle. The logic used has echoes of the sports boycott campaigns during the anti-apartheid struggle when the mantra was:

> no normal sport in an abnormal society.

This approach should be particularly effective with South African artists. Theirs was a society that imposed the same kind of restrictions and segregationist policies currently pursued by Israel towards Palestinians.

But some artists have responded by arguing that they don't get involved in politics. Or, they claim that their politics require that they treat all audiences equally. Some argue that music and art are forces that bring people together and therefore play a positive role regardless of politics.

These claims do not address the core issue: performing in a society experiencing intense conflict, against the wishes of a central constituency, which is largely prevented from attending, is itself a political statement.

Whether they intend it or not, artists who defy the boycott call are aligning themselves with the oppressive Israeli regime.

A common objection to this argument is that there are many oppressive regimes of various kinds, and that there's therefore no reason to single out Israel for special treatment.

While the first part of this argument is true, the second doesn't follow. The call to boycott Israel as a destination for artists, academics, sports people and cultural activists, does not stem from its oppressive policies as such. It stems from the fact that Israel runs a regime that amounts to what I've described as an apartheid of a special type.

Although not identical to the South African version, it meets the definition of apartheid in international law:

> an institutionalised regime of systematic oppression and domination by one racial group over any other racial group or groups and committed with the intention of maintaining that regime.

In specific terms, Palestinian residents of the West Bank and Gaza, forcibly dominated by Israel since 1967, cannot vote in elections to Israeli representative institutions. They have no say in the way they are ruled by Israel, cannot move, trade and engage in normal economic activity freely. Their land, water and natural resources are controlled by Israel, which uses them to benefit its own (Jewish) citizens at their expense.

Needless to say, Palestinians couldn't attend DJ Black Coffee's performance in Tel Aviv. Only 15% of the overall Palestinian population have Israeli citizenship and access to basic political rights. They too are subject to a range of formal and informal discriminatory mechanisms.

The Role of Boycotts

What role can culture play in global solidarity campaign against Israel?

Boycotting academic, cultural and sports activities in Israel is an essential part. But total avoidance may not be the most useful political strategy. It should be combined with activities that take place as part of political dissent and resistance efforts from within the country.

For example, a number of possible contributions can be made to Palestinian cultural freedom struggle. These can take a number of forms such as invitations to perform and exhibit, alternative funding to allow independence from state support, and activities that would help cultural workers to organise locally and spread their messages globally.

This can be done by:

- Forging links with Palestinians and Israeli artists, performers and academics, who follow progressive programmes of action, and

- Renouncing any links with the Israeli state and its funding mechanisms.

This would allow for an effective counter to official policies of segregation and the isolation of critical voices.

The BDS Movement Is Worse Than Ineffective

Philip Mendes

In the following viewpoint, Philip Mendes writes that the BDS movement grew out of the second Palestinian intifada, an uprising that occurred as a result of Israel's attempt to fight back against terrorism. In contrast to those who support a two-state solution for Israel and Palestine, BDS favors a one-state solution, where Palestinians will prevail and Jews will be marginalized. The goal of BDS, therefore, is the elimination of the Jewish state as we know it. In conducting itself the way it has, the BDS movement has not only been ineffective economically and socially, but it has had the opposite effect it intended: BDS has led to a strengthening of the Israeli hard right wing. Mendes directs the Social Inclusion and Social Policy Research Unit in the Department of Social Work at Monash University in Melbourne, Australia. He is the author or co-author of seven books, including Jews and Australian Politics *and* Jews and the Left: The Rise and Fall of a Political Alliance.

As you read, consider the following questions:

1. According to the viewpoint, what was the catalyst for the BDS movement?
2. What is the aim of BDS, according to the viewpoint?
3. What are the author's recommendations concerning the ongoing Palestinian-Israeli conflict?

The international boycott, divestment and sanctions (BDS) campaign against Israel was a by-product of the second Palestinian Intifada and the collapse of the Oslo Peace Process. In April and May, 2002, groups of academics in Europe and Australia urged a boycott of all Israeli academics and academic institutions. The timing of these initiatives was instructive: They commenced immediately following the height of the Palestinian suicide bombing attacks in March, 2002, which killed sixty-three Israelis and injured many hundreds. These attacks provoked Israel's invasion of the leading West Bank cities in an attempt to destroy the terror networks and stop the carnage. Yet the initiators of the academic boycott campaign chose to condemn the invasion rather than the terrorism.

In April, 2004, sixty Palestinian academic and non-government organizations publicly called for an academic and cultural boycott of Israel. The BDS campaign was then formalized on July 9th, 2005 as the Palestinian Campaign for an Academic and Cultural Boycott. The campaign announced three key aims: 1) to end the Israeli occupation of lands occupied in the 1967 war, including East Jerusalem, and dismantle the security barrier; 2) to achieve full equality for the Arab-Palestinian citizens of Israel; 3) to support the rights of Palestinian refugees, including their demand for a right of return to Israel as implied by the 1948 UN Resolution 194, which followed Israel's success in the 1948 war.

The campaign has not endorsed a two-state solution that respects the national and human rights of both Israeli Jews and Palestinian Arabs. The official statements that emanate from the Palestinian Campaign for an Academic and Cultural Boycott of Israel emphasize that the first and foremost priority is to reverse the events of 1948 that led to the Palestinian refugee tragedy, and secondly, to demand the return of the 1948 Palestinian refugees and their millions of descendants to their former homes inside Green Line Israel.

The leading Palestinian BDS advocate, Omar Barghouti, in his 2011 book *BDS: the Global Struggle for Palestinian Rights*, is completely honest about his real intentions. He explicitly vilifies Palestinian moderates and Israeli leftists (such as Uri Avnery) who support two states, and he even opposes a binational state based on parity between the two national groups. Rather, Barghouti bizarrely returns to the long-obsolete PLO proposal for a secular democratic state that recognizes Jews only as a religious, not national, community.

To me, this amounts to calling for the elimination of the existing State of Israel. Even as harsh a critic of Israel as Noam Chomsky has excoriated the BDS movement for its lack of support for Israel's right to exist and for misleading the Palestinian people.

In Great Britain, the BDS movement has been openly McCarthyist. The Association of University Teachers, for example — now amalgamated into the University and College Union, UCU — has proposed the exemption from the boycott of "good" Israeli academics who are willing to condemn the policies of Israel and conform to a test of political orthodoxy.

Britain's UCU has also been implicitly if not explicitly anti-Semitic — as acknowledged in September, 2007, when it withdrew its boycott campaign based on legal advice that it was an infringement of anti-discrimination legislation. The UCU has also distributed racist material that includes conspiracy theories concerning alleged Jewish control of New Labour and international finance. This has provoked accusations of institutionalized anti-Semitism within the UCU, legal threats to sue the UCU on grounds of discrimination, and the mass resignations of Jewish members. One of the few remaining Jewish UCU members, Ronnie Fraser, told the May 2011 Union Congress that they, "as a group of mainly white, non-Jewish trade unionists, do not have the right to tell me, a Jew, what feels like anti-Semitism and what does not."

The UCU also invited South African trade unionist Bongani Masuku, who had earlier threatened South African Jews who supported Israel with violence or expulsion, to address a union forum in favour of BDS. Masuku's comments had been formally condemned as hate speech by the South African Human Rights

Commission. It is unimaginable that the UCU would have similarly invited a white South African who had incited hatred against Black and Muslim South Africans.

Nevertheless, the UCU has rejected and denounced the European Monitoring Center on Racism and Xenophobia's widely used definition of anti-Semitism on the grounds that criticism of Israel cannot possibly be anti-Semitic. This is patently absurd.

These incidents confirm that BDS campaigns can and almost certainly will lead to the promotion of political anti-Semitism because they fundamentally target not only the occupation policies of Israel but its very right to exist. An arguable exception to this rule is the relatively new, targeted boycott of products and companies doing business with Jewish settlers in the Occupied Territories — a campaign that originated in Israel itself, with the refusal of leading Jewish cultural figures to perform or present in the settlements. This campaign has been endorsed by several rabbis as well as a few American Zionist leaders such as Peter Beinart, and has backing among some liberal Christian church groups. Intentionally or not, however, it gives legitimation to the BDS movement as a whole. To me, a Zionist BDS is a contradiction in terms, for the BDS movement is anti-Zionist — just as the West Bank settlement project is anti-Palestinian.

On the surface, BDS appears to have achieved some success in isolating Israel by attracting support from legal experts, literary figures, musicians, filmmakers, churches, trade unions, and other non-government organizations. In the academic arena, there is some evidence of academics cancelling proposed joint projects with Israeli colleagues, refusing requests for research cooperation, and refusing to attend conferences in Israel. There has also been some specific banning of individual Israeli academics and scholars from international conferences.

However, no major college or university has endorsed the boycott, no American university has voted to divest Israeli shares, and a much greater number of academics internationally have signed anti-boycott rather than pro-boycott petitions. Most

BDS and Racism

In a guest editorial in the Toronto Sun, Stephen Ellis claimed that the anti-Israel boycott, divestment and sanctions (BDS) movement was an "anti-racist" campaign that would "gain momentum." Nothing could be further from the truth. During the past two years, BDS has been forcefully rejected by students at the University of Waterloo, University of Toronto, McGill University and the University of British Columbia.

Students at Canada's top institutions can see right through the absurd claims being made by Ellis and his comrades. Far from being anti-racist, BDS is the definition of racism.

To boycott an entire nationality of people, including athletes, artists and professors—because of political disagreements with their government—is clearly bigoted and counter-productive. In fact, the failures of the BDS movement are so apparent that, even the Palestinian Authority, led by Mahmoud Abbas, has repeatedly refused to adopt it. If Palestinians are ignoring a campaign supposedly waged on their behalf, why do its western acolytes persist?

The hard reality is that the BDS movement is not motivated by a sincere desire to make things better for Palestinians, but rather a perverse drive to make things worse for Israelis and Jews around the world. This hateful attitude is on perfect display in the saga surrounding Ontario teacher Nadia Shoufani. Ellis tells us that she simply "spoke in favour of Palestinian rights." In fact, Shoufani publicly hailed Samir Kuntar, a terrorist who smashed the skull of a 4-year-old Israeli girl against a rock, along with Ghassan Kanafani, who helped to plan a 1972 massacre at an Israeli airport in which 26 innocent people were murdered.

Apparently, for BDS advocates, "Palestinian rights" includes the right to murder Jews at will. For Canadian journalists to highlight this nonsense isn't "shameful"—it's just good journalism, and Sun columnist Sue-Ann Levy should be commended for it, not condemned.

At B'nai Brith Canada, we won't allow support for terrorism to go unchallenged. We will continue to expose the hypocrisy of former Pink Floyd frontman Roger Waters, who is angered by Jewish boycotts of his own concerts even as he urges the boycott of Israeli musicians. And we will continue to expose the vicious and anti-Semitic agenda behind the BDS movement, no matter the cost.

"Guest Column: BDS Is a Dismal Failure," by Michael Mostyn, Postmedia Network Inc.,
October 23, 2017.

importantly, no Western government has endorsed a boycott, which is crucial both for Israel's international political standing and its ability to maintain normal trade relations.

As a result, the BDS campaign has had little if any effect on key political and trade relations. It has had no impact whatsoever in regards to achieving its key political aims, or more generally in securing Israeli political or territorial concessions. On the contrary, by targeting all Israelis as the political enemy and reinforcing a siege mentality, BDS seems to be one of a number of factors that are strengthening the Israeli right wing. BDS gives no encouragement whatsoever to those Israelis seeking to negotiate a two-state solution based on mutual compromise with the Palestinians. Instead, the zero-sum nature of the BDS agenda guarantees never-ending conflict, for Israeli Jews will never unilaterally surrender and concede their national existence.

By now, most Jewish organizations worldwide have stated their support for a two-state solution based on the continuing existence of the State of Israel and the creation of a neighboring Palestinian State—but many of these organizations damn the plan with silence these days, as the Netanyahu government has shown little intent to pursue the two-state solution, despite its being official Israeli policy. Nevertheless, given that before the 1993 Oslo agreements, neither the Israeli government nor most Jewish groups even recognized Palestinian national rights, this is quite a remarkable turn-around.

The question remains, however, as to whether this major evolution in official Israeli and Jewish opinion is reflected in action. Even Jews outside of Israel should feel challenged, now, to define what we mean by a two-state solution, including the extent of territorial withdrawal from the West Bank we think acceptable, and to outline the concrete strategies we are willing to support to promote this outcome.

In fact, current Israeli policies and actions—or inaction—play into the hands of the BDS campaign. The Israeli government claims that it wants to negotiate a two-state solution and is waiting for a suitable Palestinian partner willing to accommodate Israel's security requirements. In practice, however, the government has failed to promote progress towards a two-state solution, and has only strengthened the Greater Israel project. Apart from the short-lived freeze on the extension of existing settlements, it has done absolutely nothing to reverse the growing presence of Jewish settlers far beyond the Green Line (that is, pre-1967) borders. The government has even talked about legalizing outposts built on private Palestinian land, and Foreign Minister Avigdor Lieberman actually lives in such a settlement, Nokdim, south of Bethlehem, well outside Israel's recognized borders.

Such settlements are a problem precisely because they were built to prevent the creation of a contiguous Palestinian state alongside Israel. This remains the case, irrespective of what the Palestinians say or do. We all know that there are massive barriers to peace on the Palestinian side: the absolutism of their political culture; the continued demands for a literal rather than symbolic return of 1948 refugees to Israel; and the still-growing influence of Hamas, a racist, fundamentalist group that opposes any coexistence with Israel and uses violence as a first resort. Yet just as the Palestinians have choices to make regarding actions that either resolve or prolong the conflict, so do the Israelis.

I would recommend the following. The new Israeli coalition government should take advantage of its flexible political power to issue a statement that it plans to dismantle all Jewish settlements east of the security barrier over the next five years. This would require some seventy thousand settlers to be evacuated. The precise details for the implementation of the plan should be negotiated with the Palestinian Authority and the international community, and time should be allowed for all those settlers to be paid adequate compensation and find suitable housing within Green Line Israel. In addition, the government should state that Israeli troops will remain in place in the West Bank until such time as the Palestinian Authority, preferably with the assistance of an international peace-keeping force (as Mahmoud Abbas himself has suggested), can demonstrate its ability to maintain a peaceful border with Israel.

The vast majority of settlers will remain in the larger settlement blocs—which constitute about 8.6 per cent of the West Bank, including forty-nine settlements and 190,000 settlers—with the long-term aim of exchanging this territory with the Palestinians for appropriate territory inside Israel.

Such a proposal would conclusively demonstrate that the Israeli people are committed to making the significant concessions required for a two-state solution, and would place the onus on the Palestinians to demonstrate their own willing to compromise. It would certainly defang the BDS campaign by reminding everybody that both sides have to give significant ground if there is to be a resolution to the conflict.

The BDS Movement Is Effective and Right

Donna Nevel and Dorothy M. Zellner

In the following viewpoint, Donna Nevel and Dorothy M. Zellner argue that the harsh realities of the Palestinian occupation have necessitated a strong response, and BDS is that response. It is an ethical response to an intolerable situation. The authors contend that BDS is working, as more and more countries, corporations, and institutions join the boycott, divest from Israeli institutions, or sanction Israel. BDS is meant to force Israel to review the Palestinian situation and to come up with a reasonable response, whether it is a two-state solution or something else. The authors believe Israel should stop calling BDS anti-Semitic or a tactic for the destruction of Israel and work to resolve the Palestinian dilemma. Nevel and Zellner are activists for Palestinian-Israeli peace and justice and founding members of Jews Say No!, a New York-based group working to improve the Israeli government's policies toward the Palestinians.

As you read, consider the following questions:

1. What is the actual situation of Palestinians under Israeli control, according to the authors?
2. Why is BDS an ethical and necessary response to the situation?
3. How is BDS growing?

As Jewish activists working to end the Israeli occupation of Palestine, we take exception to Philip Mendes' criticism of Boycott, Divestment and Sanctions (BDS) in "Why BDS is Ineffective and Worse: But the Issue of Palestinian National Rights Will Not Go Away" (Summer, 2012).

Mendes says not a single word about the realities of life for Palestinians living under occupation. Here are some of them:

- Palestinians are denied basic human rights: Israel has built a so-called "separation" wall that takes approximately 15 percent of Palestinian land, locking them in. Israel has created hundreds of checkpoints, where Palestinians are routinely harassed and humiliated, inside Palestine and at the borders; a separate roadway system for Israelis and Palestinians; and a permit system for Palestinians to secure entrance to Jerusalem and obtain necessary medical treatment at Israeli hospitals. Israeli army forays into Jenin and other cities are routine.

- Israel controls the air space, commerce, and water and electricity supplies in the West Bank and Gaza, as well the outlets to the Mediterranean Sea.

- Israel holds nearly five thousand Palestinian prisoners, many not charged with any crime and without access to legal assistance.

- As a result of Israeli government occupation policies, approximately five hundred thousand settlers reside in the West Bank, Gaza, and East Jerusalem (illegally under international law, since they are living on land that is not theirs). This has involved extensive expropriation of Palestinian land, demolition of Palestinians' homes, and uprooting of their olive trees.

Palestinians are a civilian population, and unlike Israel, have no army, navy, aircraft, airport, missiles, drones, tanks, jeeps, helicopters, tear gas grenades, "stink" bombs, or sound bombs. The

Palestinian resistance takes place in the face of extreme violence perpetrated by the Israeli government.

Space limitations prevent us from elaborating on additional problems, but these include widespread discrimination against Palestinian citizens of Israel and the terrible effect of the occupation on Israeli society itself.

More than twenty years have gone by since Oslo and the situation has only gotten worse. The US government, Israel's staunchest ally and supporter, funds Israel (with our tax money) to the tune of at least $3 billion a year and makes toothless criticisms of the settlements and the occupation.

Given this situation, BDS is a necessary and ethical response to an illegal and brutal occupation. Period.

Is BDS ineffective, as Mendes says? No. BDS is growing. In the eight years since hundreds of Palestinian civil society organizations called for BDS—similarly to the boycott/divest movement against South African apartheid—Norway, Sweden and Holland have pulled their retirement funds from Israeli companies, and pressure is now on for US retirement funds like TIAA-CREF to divest from companies that support the occupation. In May, the United Methodist Church voted overwhelmingly to boycott settlement goods, and, in the Presbyterian Church, the vote for divestment lost by the narrowest margin of 333 to 331, with two abstentions.

There is also support for boycott in the Jewish community and in Israel itself, which ranges from support for full boycott of all Israeli products to boycott of settlement projects. Some sixty leading Israeli actors and playwrights recently refused to play in the new theatre in Ariel, one of Israel's largest settlements, and were supported by one hundred and fifty leading Israeli academics and writers when they were attacked by the Israeli government. An Israeli organization, Boycott from Within, organizes for BDS. Jewish Voice for Peace, which continues to grow across the US, focuses on boycott and divestment campaigns that directly target Israel's occupation of the West Bank and East Jerusalem and its blockade of the Gaza Strip. Partners for Peace in Israel (formerly

The BDS Movement and Academic Freedom

Coming on the heels of several spectacular successes of the Palestinian Campaign for the Academic and Cultural Boycott of Israel (PACBI) and its global partners in recent months, the unanimous position taken by the National Council of the American Studies Association (ASA) endorsing the academic boycott of Israel provides fresh evidence that the boycott, divestment and sanctions (BDS) movement may be reaching a tipping point on college campuses and academic associations. Already, the Israeli government is treating the movement as a "strategic" threat and US Secretary of State John Kerry has labeled it as an "existential danger" to Israel.

The academic and cultural boycott is part of the BDS movement, which represents the overwhelming majority in Palestinian society and seeks to realize basic Palestinian rights under international law through applying effective, global, morally consistent pressure on Israel and all the institutions that collude in its violations of international law, as was done against apartheid South Africa.

As Judith Butler describes it, "The BDS movement has become the most important contemporary alliance calling for an end to forms of citizenship based on racial stratification, insisting on rights of political self-determination for those for whom such basic freedoms are denied or indefinitely suspended, insisting as well on substantial ways of redressing the rights of those forcibly and/or illegally dispossessed of property and land."

"On Academic Freedom and the BDS Movement," by Omar Barghouti, The Nation, December 14, 2013.

Meretz USA) and Americans for Peace Now have endorsed the settlement boycott.

In any case, BDS cannot be judged by economic success alone; it is a potent international political tactic.

And why, according to Mendes, is BDS worse than ineffective? His major objection to BDS is that he thinks it seeks the destruction of Israel, an argument that rests on one of the campaign's demands—the right of return (the others are ending the occupation, dismantling the wall, and full equality for Palestinian citizens of Israel). In fact, the equation of the right of return with the destruction of Israel is as emotionally overwrought as it is misleading. There is general agreement among historians, including Israelis, that approximately seven hundred and fifty thousand Palestinians were expelled from their homes. International law gives them an indisputable right to return. That is the starting point of any discussion. Does that mean ending state policies that are anti-democratic, and insisting on a state based on equal rights for all — principles on which presumably all of us agree? Yes, that's what it means. There are lots of possibilities for what that might look like, and no shortage of creative minds and committed people to make that happen. But, unless one wants to ignore history or international law or fairness/justice, the starting point is the right of return.

Further, in his discussion of the two-state solution, Mendes says it is being embraced now by most Jewish organizations and by the Israeli government (though he admits the "Netanyahu government has shown little intent to pursue [it], despite its being official Israeli policy"). It seems ironic (and worse) that, after massive settlement expansion has eaten up much of Palestinian land and destroyed any contiguous land mass, the Israeli government is now supposedly talking about two states. What Mendes fails to mention is that as far back as the late 1980s when a wide range of Palestinian leaders and Israeli and US Jewish peace leaders were having these very discussions based on self-determination for both peoples, it was members of the Jewish establishment and the Israeli government, not the Palestinian movement, who opposed it. (One of us participated in these discussions.)

Our immediate solution? Open up genuine discussions in the Jewish communities around the world about the occupation, the wall, and the right of return. Stop the tactics of calling one's opponents anti-Semitic or claiming that they advocate the "elimination of Israel" when they are simply examining problems that must be addressed to eliminate injustice and uphold our tradition of "Justice, justice thou shalt pursue."

Long term, whether there is one state or two states or a federation of states or some kind of binational arrangement, what matters is that it must be a just solution based on equal rights and respect and safety for all. Until that happens, BDS is here to stay.

Periodical and Internet Sources Bibliography

The following articles have been selected to supplement the diverse views presented in this chapter.

Ali Al-Arian, "Why Does Israel Fear the BDS Movement So Much?" *Aljazeera*, January 8, 2018. https://www.aljazeera.com/blogs /americas/2018/01/israel-fear-bds-movement-180108135253899 .html.

Nora Barrows-Friedman, "What Were the Top BDS Victories of 2017?" *Electronic Intifada*, December 28, 2017.https:// electronicintifada.net/blogs/nora-barrows-friedman/what-were -top-bds-victories-2017.

Dr. Mordechai Kedar, "The BDS Movement Is in Trouble," *Arutz Sheva*, July 19, 2017. http://www.israelnationalnews.com /Articles/Article.aspx/20061.

Sarah Lazare, "Ten Years On, the Undeniable, Growing Power of the BDS Movement," *Common Dreams*, July 7, 2015. https://www .commondreams.org/news/2015/07/07/ten-years-undeniable -growing-power-bds-movement.

Yousef Munayyer, "5 Reasons BDS Is Actually Working," *Nation*, July 9, 2015. https://www.thenation.com/article/5-reasons-bds-is -actually-succeeding.

Armin Rosen, "Is the BDS Movement Failing? Depends on Your Definition of Success," *Tablet*. http://www.tabletmag.com /scroll/251691/is-the-bds-movement-failing-depends-on-your -definition-of-success.

Lila Sarick, "FEATURE: Has the BDS Movement Been Effective?" *Canadian Jewish News,* March 18, 2015. http://www.cjnews.com /culture/jewish-learning/feature-bds-movement-effective.

Brian Schrauger, "How Effective Have the BDS Efforts Against Israel Been?" *Israel Today*, July 8, 2016. http://www.israeltoday.co.il /NewsItem/tabid/178/nid/29361/Default.aspx.

CHAPTER 3

How Have Countries Worldwide Responded to BDS?

In Canada the Government Must Hold Israel Responsible for Human Rights Violations

Julie Lévesque

In February of 2017, the Canadian Parliament voted overwhelmingly to condemn the BDS movement. In the following viewpoint Julie Lévesque argues that this vote was the height of hypocrisy and shows a disregard for human rights and international law. While Canada has condemned numerous countries around the world, they have let Israel go scot-free for more serious violations. Lévesque goes on to list the countries that Canada has sanctioned for various infractions. She argues that none of these countries have violated international law or committed crimes against humanity, to the extent that Israel has. Canada has failed miserably in its duty to protect human rights. Lévesque is a journalist and researcher with the Centre for Research on Globalization (CRG), Montreal. She was among the first independent journalists to visit Haiti in the wake of the January 2010 earthquake. In 2011, she was on board "The Spirit of Rachel Corrie," the only humanitarian vessel that penetrated Gaza territorial waters.

"Anti-BDS Motion—Why Does Canada Sanction Other Countries for Human Rights Violations but Not Israel?" by Julie Lévesque, Mondialisation.ca, February 26, 2016. Reprinted by permission.

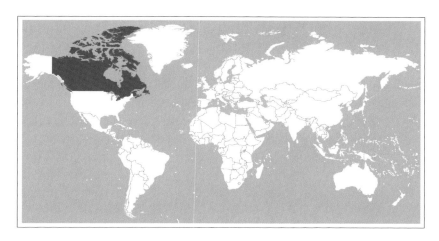

As you read, consider the following questions:

1. Why does the author reject the notion of friendship between Canada and Israel?
2. How has Israel violated international law in more serious ways than countries Canada has actually condemned?
3. How, according to the author, is Canada's vote the height of hypocrisy?

This week, the Canadian Parliament overwhelmingly voted in favour of a motion condemning the Boycott, Divestment and Sanctions (BDS) movement against Israel.

The motion, passed on February 22 by a 229-51 vote, states:

> That, given Canada and Israel share a long history of friendship as well as economic and diplomatic relations, the House reject the Boycott, Divestment and Sanctions (BDS) movement, which promotes the demonization and delegitimization of the State of Israel, and call upon the government to condemn any and all attempts by Canadian organizations, groups or individuals to promote the BDS movement, both here at home and abroad.

First, there is no such thing as "friendship" between states. States have no friends, they have interests and nothing else.

Second, the BDS movement does not promote "the demonization and delegitimization of the State of Israel," as the motion puts it, in a very unfactual and questionable manner. The BDS movement promotes international law and Palestinian rights and condemns Israel's total lack of respect for both.

Despite its emotional and propagandist wording, the motion completely fails to hide the fact that it condemns criticism of human rights violations by Israel. This calls for some explanations.

By condemning a peaceful movement that tries to bring Israel to account, Canada expresses its total disregard for human rights and international law and its sheer hypocrisy when faced with human rights violations.

There are currently 22 states targeted by Canadian sanctions, several of them for human rights violations. And Israel, being Canada's "friend", is not one of them, even if the sanctioned countries' misdeeds pale in comparison to the death and destruction Israel has imposed on Palestinians for decades.

While not one sanction has been imposed on Israel for its war crimes and crimes against humanity, some countries have been sanctioned by Canada simply for "misappropriating state funds."

There are no words to describe the scale of this hypocrisy, but, we don't need any since the facts speak for themselves. Before looking at the list of sanctioned countries and the reasons behind their sanctions, it is worth mentioning only a few facts about Israel.

As mentioned in the quote above, Israel's policies and practices violate the most fundamental human rights of the Palestinians. The Hebrew state has been the subject of at least 77 UN resolutions since 1955, and has been criticized in at least 26 resolutions for its violations of U.N. Security Council resolutions.

In July 2015, a report by Amnesty International found "compelling evidence of serious violations of international humanitarian law by Israeli forces" as well as "strong evidence of war crimes and possible crimes against humanity" during Israel's 2014 assault on Gaza." Evidence of war crimes and crimes against humanity were also found during Operation Cast Lead in 2008.

Of course, most reports from the U.N. as well as the ones from human rights organizations mentioned below pretend to be "balanced" by equally blaming both sides, the Israeli army as well as Palestinian militias. If opinions can be "balanced", facts, however, cannot, and the scale of death and destruction doesn't lie. Most, if not all the damage and loss of life occurs on the Palestinian side. Every single time.

These few facts about Operations Cast Lead in 2008 and Protective Edge in 2014 prove it:

Cast Lead:

Between 1,385 and 1,419 Palestinians were killed during Cast Lead, a majority of them civilians, including at least 308 minors under the age of 18. More than 5000 more were wounded. Thirteen Israelis were also killed, including 3 civilians.

According to the UN, 3,540 housing units were completely destroyed, with another 2,870 sustaining severe damage.

More than 20,000 people—many of them already refugees, some two or three times over—were made homeless.

Protective Edge:

At least 2,100 Palestinians were killed, of whom the United Nations identified more than 1,500 as civilians, and approximately 11,000 people, mostly civilians, were injured. The tens of thousands of Israeli attacks caused the vast majority of destruction during the fighting, which left uninhabitable 22,000 homes, displacing 108,000 people, and left hundreds of thousands without adequate water or electricity.

Attacks by Palestinian civilians injured 61 Israeli settlers in the West Bank as of October 31, the UN reported. In addition to the three Israeli teenagers who were killed in June, nine Israeli civilians were killed by Palestinians.

How many dead Israeli civilians compared to Palestinian civilians? How many housing units destroyed in Israel? How many

Ontario's Parliament Rejects BDS

The Legislative Assembly of Ontario on Thursday passed by a vote of 49-5 a historic motion affirming the Ontario Legislature's rejection of the anti-Israel Boycott, Divestment and Sanctions (BDS) movement.... "That, in the opinion of this House, the Legislative Assembly of Ontario should; stand firmly against any position or movement that promotes or encourages any form of hatred, hostility, prejudice, racism and intolerance in any way; recognize the longstanding, vibrant and mutually beneficial political, economic and cultural ties between Ontario and Israel, built on a foundation of shared liberal democratic values; endorse the Ottawa Protocol on Combating Anti-Semitism; and reject the differential treatment of Israel, including the Boycott, Divestment and Sanctions movement," the motion read.

Martow told the House Speaker that Canadian universities have become battlegrounds of intolerance and that Canadian students incur hostility and demonization of Israel that affects their psychological well-being. "We wouldn't be supporting the KKK, so why are we allowing BDS organizations to hold anti-Israel demonstrations on campuses?" Martow asked, adding, "BDS want to hide behind freedom of speech. BDS is boycotting not just Israel, but all Jews and other supporters of Israel." She concluded her argument by urging everyone to "stand up and say no to intolerance against Jewish people".

A bill designed to prevent the Ontario government from conducting business with companies that support a boycott of Israel failed to pass at the Ontario Legislature on May 19, 2016. The bill identified the BDS movement as "one of the main vehicles for spreading anti-Semitism and the delegitimization of Israel globally and is increasingly promoted on university campuses in Ontario ... leading to intimidation and violence on campuses." It called on the province, as well as on colleges and universities, to abstain from doing business with companies that support the BDS movement.

Ontario Premier Kathleen Wynne later said she wanted to work with members of the opposition to draft a new motion on the issue which would be "less divisive". In February, the Canadian parliament approved by a large majority a draft resolution rejecting and condemning the BDS movement.

"Ontario's parliament overwhelmingly rejects BDS," Dalit Halevi, Arutz Sheva, February 16, 2016.

homeless Israelis? Let's be honest. A truly balanced report would reflect the facts and not try to equally blame both sides. The forces in this conflict as well as the damage done are anything but equal. They are completely disproportionate.

That being said, Israel's contempt for international law is legend and with this motion, Canadian Parliamentarians have just proven one more time they are bought and sold.

It is now worth taking a look at the countries against which Canada has placed sanctions and why, since all of them, without exception, pale in comparison to Israel's bloody record.

The list clearly shows how Canada has no credibility whatsoever when it comes to condemning states for their lack of respect for human rights or people who protest against criminal states, for that matter.

Here is the list of the countries sanctioned for human rights reasons. It should be noted that several, if not all, background explanations provided on the Canadian Government web site (in brackets) are totally biased and simplistic, when not pure propaganda.

Belarus: "[D]eteriorating human rights situation."

> This includes "widespread harassment and detention of opposition party campaign workers, the physical assault of senior opposition figures, arbitrary use of state powers to support the incumbent president, pressure on state workers and students to support the President, restrictions on the ability of opposition campaigns to communicate with the electorate, and control of the state media to severely restrict access by opposition candidates.
>
> What happens in the Occupied Territories is much worse, yet no sanctions against Israel.

Burma: "[G]ravity of the human rights and humanitarian situation…, which threatened peace and security in the entire region."

Libya: "[V]iolence and the use of force against civilians."

> Day-to-day in the Occupied Territories.

Russia: "Activists were beaten, kidnapped and tortured [in Ukraine]. The Russian government encouraged, and supported, these measures."

Meanwhile, more and more "Palestinian children [are] beaten and tortured by Israeli security forces while in detention." Read also Israeli NGO B'Tselem's report Backed by the System: Abuse and Torture at the Shikma Interrogation Facility.

Sudan: "[H]umanitarian crisis and widespread human rights violations resulting from the conflict in Darfur region"

Syria: "The Syrian Government's violent crackdown on peaceful protesters led to many civilian deaths and injuries. Thousands of civilians were detained arbitrarily and there were credible reports of summary executions and torture."

Israel arbitrarily detains Palestinians on a regular basis, including children, and summary executions and torture and common.

According to B'Tselem: "At the end of Dec. 2015, 422 Palestinian minors were held in Israeli prisons as security detainees and prisoners, including 6 administrative detainees."

According to Human Rights Watch:

Israeli security forces continued to arrest children suspected of criminal offenses, usually stone-throwing, in their homes at night, at gunpoint; question them without a family member or lawyer present; and coerce them to sign confessions in Hebrew, which they do not understand... As of October 31, Israel held 457 Palestinian administrative detainees without charge or trial, based on secret evidence. Israeli prison authorities shackled hospitalized Palestinians to their hospital beds after they went on long-term hunger strikes to protest their administrative detention.

Last year, Amnesty International has condemned "what it called a 'clear pattern' of... summary killings... as the number of Palestinians killed by Israeli forces this month [October 2015] rose to at least 61.

Ukraine: "Activists were beaten, kidnapped and tortured."

Zimbabwe: "marked escalation in human rights violations and violence directed at the political opposition, a stolen election, the denial of a peaceful democratic transition and a worsening humanitarian situation."

Other reasons for which Canada has sanctioned countries include:

- "political crisis and conflict" (Yemen, Somalia);
- "violations of ceasefire and hostilities" (Ivory Coast, Democratic Republic of the Congo);
- "misappropriated state funds" (Egypt, Tunisia);
- "heavy loss of human life and widespread material damage resulting from a conflict" (Eritrea, Somalia);
- "nuclear program" (Sanctions on Iran, which has a nonexistent nuclear program, but none on Israel, which is known to possess between 200 and 400 nuclear warheads.)
- "invasion" (Sanctions on Iraq for the invasion of Kuwait… but no sanctions for the US which has illegally invaded Iraq, among other countries, and of course, no sanctions on Israel for decades of occupation);
- "continued escalation of hostilities" (Lebanon)
- "support for the Revolutionary United Front in Sierra Leone" (Liberia)
- "violation of the constitution and international law" (Ukraine).
- "conducting a test of a nuclear weapon" (North Korea)
- "acts of violence and the increase in acts of piracy and armed robbery at sea against vessels" (Somalia)
- "engaging in violent conflict, much of it along ethnic lines" (South Sudan)

As you probably noticed, none of these countries has been accused of war crimes or crimes against humanity.

Canada imposes sanctions on countries for misappropriated state funds, but regards war criminal state Israel as a "friend" which deserves that it condemns its own citizens for protesting against its supreme crime.

Parliamentarians need to explain this nonsense.

As a member of the United Nations, Canada should, as stated in the U.N. Preamble, "reaffirm faith in fundamental human rights, in the dignity and worth of the human person, in the equal rights of men and women and of nations large and small, and… establish conditions under which justice and respect for the obligations arising from treaties and other sources of international law can be maintained."

By voting in favour of this motion, Canadian Parliamentarians have failed to honor their obligations. Miserably.

In France Actions Against the BDS Boycott Are Justified

Freddy Eytan

In the following viewpoint, Ambassador Freddy Eytan responds favorably to the French government's vote to label BDS activities as hate crimes and to ban BDS in France. Eytan argues that the BDS movement is anti-Semitic and that it is violent and hateful. He cites numerous anti-Semitic hate crimes in France as evidence that BDS supporters are not the peaceful petitioners that they make themselves out to be. Eytan calls on the three major economic powers in Europe, Great Britain, France, and Germany to be vigilant in their rejection of the hate and violence associated with BDS. Eytan is a former Foreign Ministry senior advisor who served in Israel's embassies in Paris and Brussels and was Israel's first Ambassador to the Islamic Republic of Mauritania. He was also the spokesman of the Israeli delegation in the peace process with the Palestinians. He has also published biographies of Shimon Peres, Ariel Sharon, Benjamin Netanyahu, as well as The 18 Who Built Israel.

As you read, consider the following questions:

1. Why is France's vote against BDS important?
2. How is BDS a violent campaign?
3. Why is it necessary for England and Germany to follow France's actions?

"Will the French Anti-Boycott Law Lead to a Pan-European Law?" by Amb. Freddy Eytan, Jerusalem Center for Public Affairs, November 11, 2015. Reprinted by permission.

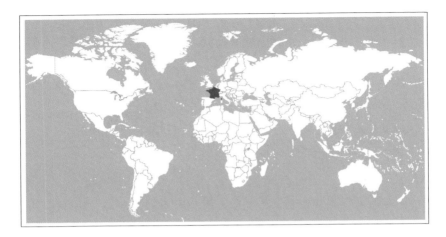

F rance's supreme appellate court, La Cour de Cassation, which is the highest court in the country, has finally made an important ruling that any activity aimed at imposing a boycott on Israel constitutes a hate crime or a clear instance of discrimination.

The ruling actually applies Article 24 of France's Law on the Freedom of the Press, which was first passed on July 29, 1881, and updated in December 2004. This law imposes imprisonment or a fine of 45,000 euros on a person or entity "that incites to discrimination, to hate or to violence against a person or a group of persons on the basis of extraction, affiliation or nonaffiliation with an ethnic group, nation, race or religion."

This October 27, 2015 ruling came in the wake of two major incidents in a huge supermarket of the Carrefour chain, located close to the town of Mulhouse in the southern part of the Alsace region in the northeast of the country.

In the first incident, which occurred on September 26, 2009, dozens of BDS activists streamed into the supermarket wearing shirts with the slogans "Long Live Palestine" and "Boycott Israel." They handed out leaflets charging that buying products from Israel means "granting legitimacy to the crimes that Israel perpetrates in the Gaza Strip," that "Israel murders innocent children," and that "The CARREFOUR chain is a collaborator."

Despite the complaints that official Jewish organizations conveyed to the French authorities, the same thing happened in the same supermarket on May 22, 2010. In both incidents the activists engaged in vandalism, throwing all Israeli products on the floor and emptying the shelves in the kosher products section without being stopped by the security guards. Most French supermarkets have a kosher-food and modesty-observing section for Jews just as they have halal sections for Muslims; in recent months the latter have greatly expanded with thousands of products. During Muslim holidays the supermarket shelves are inundated with halal products.

A local court finally convicted all those who took part in planning and perpetrating these acts, fining them a cumulative sum of 12,000 euros.

This is not the first time that activists who engage in incitement to hatred and discrimination have been convicted. The EuroPalestine organization has tried more than once, without success, to run as a political party in elections for the French parliament and even for the European Parliament. Its website has waged a mendacious and despicable anti-Israeli propaganda campaign for years. The comedian Dieudonné, who is active in a pro-Palestinian organization, has also been convicted several times for Holocaust denial, anti-Semitic statements and jokes, and for popularizing the quenelle salute among young people.

Although the BDS movement is illegal in France, it continues to receive instructions from the movement's founder, Omar Barghouti, who usually resides in London. Barghouti claims that he is operating in a democratic country where freedom of political expression is as absolute as freedom of the press. He says that the law allows him to criticize the policies of the Israeli government, and has more than once called for opposing Israel with all means including violent and armed opposition.

Thanks to the initiative of French Jewish parliamentarian Pierre Lellouche, a member of the Republican Party of former President Sarkozy, since 2003 the so-called Lellouche law has broadened the laws against racism to include discrimination against countries.

Over the years, however, French governments have capitulated to the Arab boycott, and a detailed list was even published of French companies that were "victims of the boycott." Most of the companies that were boycotted were owned or managed by Jews. In any case, it is beyond doubt that the boycott, whether on the governmental or the popular level as in the BDS case, is fueled by both tacit and open anti-Semitic motives. The funding for these activities must be stopped, and the authorities must outlaw any movement or organization that supports a racist boycott.

The recent ruling by the supreme appellate court is certainly encouraging. It establishes unequivocally that promoting the boycott of the Jewish state is a hate crime and entails incitement to discrimination. This important ruling, however, was insufficiently covered in the French media and only won headlines in Israeli newspapers.

The judges in Paris deserve praise, as do the umbrella organization of French Jewry, CRIF, and the nongovernmental organization BNCVA along with its president Sammy Ghozlan for their spirited activity. These dedicated activists constantly monitor pro-Palestinian activists for any attempts to violate the existing laws.

It is now all the more vital to work for the adoption of the French law by other European countries, such as Britain. Whoever fights anti-Semitism and racism must condemn the ugly phenomenon of the boycott in all the domains – economic, cultural, and academic. Attempts to glorify the boycott of Israel should not only be denounced but also severely punished in a deterrent fashion.

Although Europe is an important economic power, in the sphere of foreign and defense policy it is still faltering, and the major decisions in this sphere are actually made by three countries: Germany, Britain, and France. It is now their responsibility to maintain the existing status quo and prevent the boycott of Israel and its products, standing firm against the pressures exerted by pro-Palestinian organizations and movements. One may criticize the policy of the Israeli government, but one may not boycott a democratic state that is a member of the United Nations while, at the same time, exalting Islamic State as it sows death and terror. Debates at every venue — in the media or on campuses — are essential to increased understanding, and the recent debate at Oxford University showed that there are those who will listen to Israel's message. Indeed, the arguments of American Prof. Alan Dershowitz persuaded more students than the slanders and distortions of the BDS activists. Their movement opposes any peace process, incites against Jews, and maliciously sabotages any attempt at Israeli-Palestinian reconciliation.

And finally it must be noted that the ongoing Palestinian terror activity in the territories and within Israel is likely to spark anti-Jewish incitement and violence in Europe as well. It must not be forgotten that Jews have already been killed in a kosher supermarket in Paris and at the Otzar Hatorah School in Toulouse.

Hence, the authorities must be prepared to act urgently and apply the laws of enforcement and deterrence, relentlessly prosecuting all the inciters.

In Germany Big Cities Resist the BDS Movement

Christoph Strack

Since the end of World War II and the Holocaust, Germany has been particularly sensitive to hate crimes. It is a serious felony in Germany to incite hatred. While Germany was somewhat lax on BDS up to 2017, its major cities, moved by a deeper understanding of what BDS is about, have moved to ban such activities. Hate crimes and anti-Semitic behavior has been on the rise in Germany as of late, and the actual number of incidences likely far outstrips the reported numbers. Some have called for an anti-Semitism commissioner to counter such activity. Strack works for the German media company, Deutsche Welle.

As you read, consider the following questions:

1. Why have German authorities decided that BDS activities are anti-Semitic?
2. How have German cities taken actions against BDS?
3. How did incidents in Berlin trigger an anti-BDS backlash?

For over ten years, an international network of protest against Israeli policy toward the Palestinians has existed: the "Boycott, Divestment, Sanctions" (BDS) movement. It began in 2005 when numerous Palestinian organizations expressed extensive criticism of Israeli policy towards the Palestinians. Internationally, the call to

"German Cities Split with 'Anti-Semitic' BDS Boycott Movement," by Christoph Strack, Deutsche Welle, September 10, 2017. Reprinted by permission.

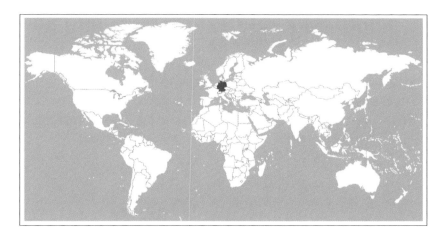

boycott Israeli products from the occupied territories and holdings of Israeli companies was based on a long-term campaign in the 1980s against the apartheid system in South Africa.

For a long time, BDS' stance was regarded as critical of Israel as a whole or anti-Zionist. But recently, several German metropolises have judged the protest movement to be "anti-Semitic" and have outlawed official support to the movement.

A few weeks ago, Frankfurt — considered Germany's business and financial capital — turned against BDS. The city's municipal authorities decided they would not allow any locations or public spaces to be used for BDS activities in the city, and they appealed to private landlords to follow suit. In addition, they announced that any associations or organizations supporting the BDS movement would see their public subsidies revoked.

"An Important Signal"

Uwe Becker, a member of Chancellor Angela Merkel's Christian Democratic Union (CDU) and a member of Frankfurt's mayoral council whose portfolio includes religious affairs, provided the impetus for the decision. He told Deutsche Welle that to him, the BDS movement is "profoundly anti-Semitic" as it uses the language "that Nazis once used" in their messaging. Moreover, he calls his city's refusal to support BDS an "important signal."

Becker said that he has received much more praise than criticism about the decision and believes that many people "have come to really understand what BDS is about."

At the national level, the anti-BDS movement is also gaining steam. At its annual convention in Essen in December 2016, Merkel's CDU party approved a petition that would make the party condemn or oppose any BDS activities. Becker also initiated that petition.

The Frankfurt alderman says he would like to see further votes of this kind. "If possible, at least the big cities in Germany and Europe should position themselves accordingly. It should become a movement." So far, he has not had any official requests to join his anti-movement movement. "But at events here and there I am already being approached informally." The topic has been brought up at the Deutscher Städtetag, a meeting of officials from over 3,400 German municipalities. It has not yet been discussed within the framework of the German-Israeli sister city network.

Munich, Berlin Follow Suit

Reaction was swift from the Bavarian capital, Munich, following Frankfurt's announcement. Several German and Israeli media reports have indicated that the city has proposed a bill that would disallow any municipal provision of space or money to pro-BDS entities.

Now Berlin has weighed in. There is, however, a back story to the Berlin Senate's distancing from the BDS movement. In June, an uproar was sparked at a Humboldt University event featuring an 82-year-old Holocaust survivor and a deputy of Israel's parliament, the Knesset. According to media reports the two were "shouted down" by BDS activists. In mid-August, a BDS-organized pro-boycott demonstration in Berlin overshadowed a pop culture festival that had received minor financing from the Israeli embassy. Various artists, mainly from the Arab world, obeyed the call to cancel their participation in the festival.

Harsh criticism of the festival boycott came first from high-ranking city officials. Berlin's mayoral council member and culture minister Klaus Lederer (The Left party) expressed horror at the outcome. "The boycott is disgusting," he said. At the national level, Germany's Minister of Cultural Affairs Monika Grütters (CDU), who supported the festival, was similarly clear. When Berlin Mayor Michael Müller (Social Democratic Party) did not initially comment, the Simon Wiesenthal Center threatened to put him on its annual anti-Semitism list, which garners high visibility internationally.

It was only after a discussion with the Central Council of Jews in Germany that Müller spoke out. "BDS stands alongside anti-Semitic signs in Berlin businesses, which are intolerable practices from the Nazi era. We will do everything possible to take spaces and money away from BDS due to its anti-Israeli hatred," he said. He expressed a desire for a "legally binding ban on providing spaces" and also mentioned the possibility of a proper ban on BDS, a step for which the interior minister, currently Thomas de Maiziere of the CDU, would be responsible. Mayor Müller thus followed Frankfurt and Munich's line. As of Friday afternoon, the BDS had not issued any response to his statements.

Reports Indicate Rising Anti-Semitism

Ultimately, these moves demonstrate that municipalities are also taking into consideration the growing concerns of many Israelis and German Jews.

On Friday, national newspaper *Die Welt* cited new federal government data on anti-Semitism. In the first half of 2017, a total of 681 such offenses were recorded, 27 more than in the same period in 2016. There was also a slight increase in cases of violence and "incitement towards hatred," which, it should be noted, has been a serious felony in Germany since the Nazi era.

Media reports also indicate that in their petition to stop funding pro-BDS entities, CDU and SPD officials in Munich cited another recent federal statistic according to which 40% of Germans hold Israel-related anti-Semitic views.

The former president of the Central Council of the Jews, Charlotte Knobloch, called the figures frightening and referred to the emergence of the anti-immigrant Alternative für Deutschland (AfD) party and the far-right, nationalist, anti-Islam Pegida movement.

Volker Beck, a Green party member of Bundestag and head of its German-Israeli Parliamentary Friendship Group, initiated the publication of the figures through an official request to the government. However, he told Die Welt, "the dark figure" [the actual or unreported figure behind a statistic — Editor's note] is "to be feared, and is probably much higher." Beck, along with various non-governmental organizations, has long been calling for an anti-Semitism commissioner to serve directly in the Federal Chancellery. In June, however, the federal government made it clear that a decision on such a representative would no longer come before the upcoming Bundestag elections. But the demand is likely to come up again after September 24.

In Israel BDS Supporters Are Blacklisted

Samuel Osborne

In the following viewpoint, Samuel Osborn reports on Israel's decision to take action against the BDS movement by publishing a list of organizations that support the boycott. Activists from these organizations will be denied entry into the country. Those supporting BDS claim that Israel's BDS Blacklist is an excuse to justify barring activists and human rights supporters and those who are justifiably concerned about Israel's treatment of the Palestinians. Israel claims that it is only fighting back against a movement that seeks to harm its citizens. Israeli officials add that they are not blacklisting those who merely criticize the country, and that other countries have also taken measures against BDS. Osborne is a reporter at the British newspaper The Independent, *where he writes about UK and worldwide news.*

As you read, consider the following questions:

1. Why has Israel acted to ban certain activists from entering the country?
2. How do opponents of this new law feel about Israel's restrictions?
3. What does Israeli official Gilad Erdan mean when he says that they have shifted from "defence to offence"?

"Israel Publishes BDS Blacklist of Organisations Banned from Entering Country, as Anti-boycott Legislation Takes Effect," by Samuel Osborne, The Independent, January 7, 2018. Reprinted by permission.

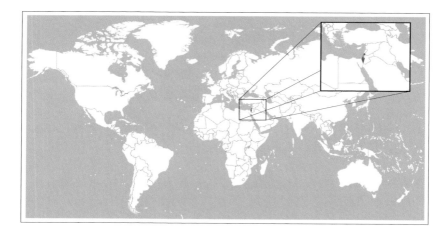

I srael has published a list of organisations supporting a boycott campaign against the country, whose activists will be banned from entering the Jewish state.

Members of 20 groups which back the Boycott, Divestment and Sanctions (BDS) movement will be denied entry visas and residency rights under a controversial law.

Gary Spedding, a British cross-party consultant on Israel and the Palestinian Territories, told The Independent the blacklist was merely an excuse to legally justify barring activists and human rights observers from entering the country.

"Israel's publishing of a 'BDS blacklist' is the latest example of just how fragile the regime actually is and demonstrates a hypersensitivity to legitimate criticisms made of the state's actions and policies vis-a-vis the Palestinians," Mr Spedding, who was refused entry to Israel in 2014, said.

"This isn't really about targeting BDS activists. It's about providing an easier legal pathway to justify refusing entry to a wide range of activists and human rights observers – many who may not even support the BDS campaign but are simply supportive of Palestinian liberty and equality.

"Activists who are determined to visit Israel and Palestine, in order to bear witness to the reality on the ground and engage with Israelis and Palestinians, should try to ensure their social media presence is minimal and that they have legitimate tourism plans to elaborate on at entry points into Israel."

The list primarily includes European and American organisations, and features the UK-based Palestine Solidarity Campaign (PSC) and War on Want, *Haaretz* reported.

Even those holding no official position within the blacklisted organisations could be denied entry, as well as mayors and politicians who promote boycotts.

"We have shifted from defence to offence," said Gilad Erdan, the minister for strategic affairs, according to *Haaretz*.

"The boycott organisations need to know that the state of Israel will act against them and not allow them to enter its territory to harm its citizens.

"No country would have allowed critics coming to harm the country to entry it."

Arye Dery, head of the interior ministry which will be responsible for implementing the list, said: "These people are trying to exploit the law and our hospitality to act against Israel and to defame the country. I will act against this by every means."

Last year, Hugh Lanning, chair of the PSC, became the first British citizen to be refused entry to Israel under the law, and Professor Kemal Hawwash, a British-Palestinian man, was also forced to fly back to the UK.

In June last year, the PSC and its supporters, including War on Want, brought a legal case against the British Government concerning guidance which restricted local councils from pursuing BDS against Israel through their pension schemes.

Campaigners argued people had a right to decide not to profit from human rights abuses, and the High Court ruled the Government had acted unlawfully by seeking to restrict "ethical" boycotts of Israel.

Israel's Strategic Affairs Ministry has been allocated $36m (£27m) for a plan to combat the BDS movement.

The plan calls for a not-for-profit organisation to be established to counter pressure the movement places on artists and companies to boycott Israel, the *Times of Israel* reports.

In a statement, the Israeli embassy in London said: "Like all other democracies, Israel will deny entrance to organisations and individuals working to undermine and harm Israel's national security. The organisations named in the list released yesterday have undertaken ongoing, consistent and significant action to promote and advance a boycott of Israel."

It said the regulation excludes political criticism of Israel as criteria for an organisation appearing on the list, and added that several other counties had taken steps to counter boycotts against Israel.

In the United States an Anti-BDS Measure Is a Bad Idea but It Is Not Unconstitutional

David Schraub

In the following viewpoint, David Schraub begins by examining claims by its opponents that the Israel Anti-Boycott Act limits free speech. But a careful, objective reading of the bill suggests that it does not. The proposed law only extends a previous law that prevents parties outside the United States from coercing US citizens into boycotting another country. The misunderstanding of this bill stems from the very nature of the BDS debate: parties on both sides are often subject to hyper-partisanship. The bill does not ban boycotts or free speech. In fact, Schraub contends, it is an unnecessary response to the situation that will not have much of an effect on the status quo. Schraub is Lecturer in Law at the University of California-Berkeley.

As you read, consider the following questions:

1. What is missing in most observer's analyses of the Israel Anti-Boycott Act?
2. How does the law distinguish between boycotting a country and boycotting a country based on an external country or organizations demands?
3. Why, according to Schraub, is this bill not worthy of the passion that it is stirring up?

"The US Anti-BDS Bill May Be Bad, but not as Bad as Some Critics Say," by David Schraub, Jewish Telegraphic Agency, July 24, 2017. Reprinted by permission.

A bill being weighed in Congress that would target boycotts of Israel and its settlements is sparking widespread outrage, especially after investigative journalist Glenn Greenwald claimed it "criminalizes free speech." The post relied on a letter from the ACLU expressing First Amendment concerns over the Israel Anti-Boycott Act. By contrast, the co-sponsors of the bill insist that it in no way hampers free speech.

So who is right?

Statutory analysis is complex under the best of circumstances, and the Israeli-Palestinian conflict does not tend to bring out people's sense of care and nuance. What has been largely missing from the discussion over the Israel Anti-Boycott Act is a close, careful reading of the bill's text and relevant statutory law — a non-hyperbolic read, but also a non-apologetic one. In short: This law has issues. It poses genuine speech concerns, and it seems to respond to a nonexistent problem.

But the more extreme claims that it bans boycotts of Israel are untrue.

A bit of background can help set the stage. While Arab countries have boycotted Israel since before there was an Israel, in the 1970s they became far more aggressive in demanding that their trading partners join them in refusing to do business with Israel. They imposed a secondary boycott whereby companies had to prove they weren't doing business with Israel in order to do business with the Arab countries.

In response, America passed a law prohibiting several actions if they were taken "with intent to comply with, further, or support any boycott fostered or imposed by a foreign country against a country which is friendly to the United States." These included:

- Discriminating against a person "on the basis of race, religion, sex, or national origin";

- Providing information "with respect to the race, religion, sex, or national origin" of any American person or their employees;

- Providing information regarding whether one had any business dealings with the boycotted country; and of course,

- Boycotting the country.

This law has been upheld against First Amendment challenges. And the most anodyne way of describing the new bill is to say it merely extends the preexisting ban on boycotting an ally of the United States at the behest of a foreign country (e.g., Qatar) to include doing so at the behest of an International Governmental Organization, or IGO (e.g., the European Union or United Nations).

Importantly, neither the current law nor the proposed one bans boycotts of Israel generally. The existing anti-boycott law only prohibits actions taken "with intent to comply with, further, or support any boycott fostered or imposed by a foreign country." Obviously, it is not generally unlawful to say whether one has business dealings with Israel. And likewise, even under this law, it is not illegal to boycott Israel — unless the reason you're doing it is to comply with a foreign country's demand that you do so.

If one says "I boycott Israel because I think Israel is terrible," that remains perfectly lawful (the ACLU is simply wrong when it suggests that the law targets those who boycott Israel "because of a political viewpoint opposed to Israeli policies"). In fact, if one says "I boycott Israel because the Palestinian Campaign for the Academic and Cultural Boycott of Israel tells me to," that's entirely lawful, too (PACBI is neither a foreign government nor an IGO). Only boycotts done at the behest of the EU or the U.N. would be newly prohibited by the law.

The ACLU's letter suggests that this represents unlawful viewpoint discrimination. But many laws are like this: They prohibit certain actions only when they are taken with a particular intent. For example, it is illegal to fire a Latino employee if one is motivated by racial prejudice against Latinos. Both the action and the intent are perfectly lawful on their own—it is not illegal to harbor racial prejudice, and it is not illegal to fire employees—but conjoined

Legislation and BDS

The Boycott, Divestment and Sanctions (BDS) movement seeks to stigmatize, delegitimize and isolate the State of Israel. BDS proponents seek to drive a wedge between Israel and the rest of the world—separating Israel's government, businesses, universities and people from their partners abroad. By manipulating the language of international law, the BDS movement depicts Israel as an illegitimate aggressor, then seeks to sanction those who interact with the Jewish state.

Why is this Legislation Needed?

In March 2016, the U.N. Human Rights Council called for the creation of a blacklist of companies conducting certain activities beyond the 1949 Armistice line, including in East Jerusalem and the Jewish Quarter of the Old City. In January 2018, the U.N. High Commissioner for Human Rights issued a pernicious report laying groundwork for utilizing the database to boycott these companies. The report threatens 206 firms— including at least 22 American companies—for actions that are completely legal under US and Israeli law.

What Action is Congress Taking to Combat the BDS Movement?

The Israel Anti-Boycott Act…would expand remaining US anti-boycott laws to international organizations like the United Nations and the European Union. Spearheaded by Sens. Ben Cardin (D-MD) and Rob

together they become illicit. One could characterize this as (to quote the ACLU's letter) punishing persons "based solely on their point of view"—the same action, taken with a different (non-prejudiced) viewpoint, is lawful—but doing so would throw the entirety of American anti-discrimination law into question.

Understanding the proposed anti-boycott measure requires grasping this distinction. Critics see provisions that target "support [for] any boycott fostered or imposed by any international governmental organization against Israel," and assume that this motive alone is being criminalized. But a close parsing of the text—and in fairness, the paragraph in question is a convoluted

Portman (R-OH), and Reps. Peter Roskam (R-IL) and Juan Vargas (D-CA), the measure also directs the US Export-Import Bank to consider BDS activity when appraising a foreign company's credit application. Introduced by Sens. Marco Rubio (R-FL) and Joe Manchin (D-WV) in the Senate and Reps. Patrick McHenry (R-NC) and Juan Vargas (D-CA) in the House, the Combating BDS Act of 2017…would grant state and local governments the right to disassociate pensions and contracts from entities that boycott, divest from or sanction Israel. The bipartisan measure would also provide federal authorization for state and local officials to take action against efforts to delegitimize the Jewish state.

Does the Israel Anti-Boycott Act Restrict Free Speech?

Nothing in the Israel-Anti-Boycott Act restricts constitutionally-protected *free speech*. The bill only regulates *commercial conduct* intended to comply with, further or support unauthorized foreign boycotts. American courts have routinely upheld federal laws restricting commerce that conflicts with US foreign policy interests as not violating free speech. Accordingly, under the proposed legislation, companies and individuals would be barred from refusing to conduct business with Israel in order to satisfy a request from the United Nations or European Union. However, they would remain entirely free to boycott Israel on their own volition.

"Oppose Boycotts of Israel, Protect US Companies," The American Israel Public Affairs Committee.

nightmare—shows that this phrase does not prohibit supporting a boycott of Israel, it only prohibits those aforementioned actions (e.g., discrimination against an employee, certifying one does no business with Israelis) if one is doing so to support a boycott call from a foreign government or, now, IGO.

But just because the hyperbolic reactions are off base does not mean that the law is worth backing. There is a legitimate free speech objection in how the law treats "support" for an IGO's announced boycott. Whereas in current law the term "support" for a boycott is modulated by terms like "comply with" or "further"—suggesting more than pure expressive sympathy—in the new bill the term "support" stands unadorned. This poses a significant risk of chilling speech because whether or not Israel boycotters are doing so because they personally find the nation terrible versus because they wish to "support" a U.N. declaration that Israel is terrible will often be quite blurry. In any event, it's not clear why that should be legally dispositive.

Other new language regarding statutory penalties — I do not believe the bill carries the risk of imprisonment, but it would be simple for its writers to to make this clear—and how "requests" for a boycott are treated also are troublesome and at the very least need reworking.

Even if these flaws were all fixed, however, there would still be a substantial difference of context: Namely, there is no serious threat that either the U.N. or the EU will call for a secondary boycott. Whereas the current law is reasonably categorized as a shield for American corporations—protecting them from being forced by foreign diktat into a boycott they do not actually endorse — this law is not responsive to any such threat.

That may or may not affect the First Amendment analysis, but it significantly undermines the law's policy rationale. Most of the litigation over the current law came because companies were providing documentation to Arab countries showing that they were boycotting Israel in order to avoid the former nations' secondary boycott. But if the U.N. or EU are not imposing a secondary boycott, there would be no occasion to furnish this information and thus virtually no situation where anyone could violate the law unless they admitted "we are boycotting Israel because the U.N. said to."

Laws can be bad without being apocalyptic and inadvisable without being unconstitutional. Discussions of Israel/Palestine, in particular, suffer from a marked propensity from people on all sides to abandon care and perspective as they race to extremes. This bill does not do the more outrageous things it stands accused of. That does not mean it is well-drafted, necessary or worth the tempest it is stirring up.

The BDS Movement Is Facing Economic Warfare

Benjamin Weinthal

In the following viewpoint, Benjamin Weinthal investigates the backlash against BDS by entities in the United States. New York governor Andrew Cuomo, for example, has come out stridently against BDS. As Weinthal explains, an economic warfare campaign against BDS, which may include political, legal, and financial pressure, can deter organizations, corporations, and governments that might otherwise participate in the BDS boycott. Additionally, there is an issue with terrorist group support of BDS that demands confrontation. While BDS activities are widespread in Europe, there are numerous economic and political opportunities for opponents to confront and weaken BDS support. Weinthal is a research fellow at the Foundation for Defense of Democracies. His writing has examined the growth of the Islamic State in Europe, growing anti-Semitism on the Continent, and neo-Nazism. Weinthals' work has appeared in The Wall Street Journal Europe, Slate, The Guardian, The New Republic, The Weekly Standard, National Review Online, *and the Israeli newspapers* Haaretz *and* The Jerusalem Post.

As you read, consider the following questions:

1. How has New York State taken action to dissuade those who might support the BDS movement?
2. Where in the United States has the BDS movement gained the most traction?
3. How does terrorist support of BDS factor into opponents efforts to blunt the movement's activities and power?

The Boycott, Divestment and Sanctions movement is staring down the barrel of economic warfare with financial assaults on BDS, replicating in many ways the sanctions architecture imposed on Iran to compel a change in its behavior over its illicit nuclear weapons program.

New York Gov. Andrew Cuomo's now-famous anti-BDS comment from last month—"It's very simple: If you boycott against Israel, New York will boycott you"—harks back to the strategy targeting European companies conducting business with Iran's regime.

European banks and firms faced being frozen out of the lucrative US market if they continued trade relations with Tehran.

Cuomo's executive order to punish companies which have state business who are engaged in BDS is part and parcel of a broader campaign unfolding in US state governments to turn BDS into a pariah movement. Robust anti-BDS legislation in Illinois coupled with State Sen. Mark Kirk's call for an investigation into German BDS bank accounts has played a critical role in disrupting BDS funding.

Commerzbank, Germany's second- largest bank, pulled the plug on a BDS account last month, a first for Europe's main economic engine.

However it is still premature to venture a guess if the Commerzbank closure will usher in account terminations among the scores of German banks that have financial relationships with BDS organizations.

While BDS is largely limited to academia in the US, Western and Central Europe is ground zero in the BDS pressure-point campaign against Israel.

New British Foreign Minister Boris Johnson, who is staunchly anti-BDS, fails to grasp the high-energy and well-organized BDS bandwidth in his backyard and on the Continent.

"I think there is some misunderstanding over here about it," Johnson said last year. "The supporters of this so-called boycott are really a bunch of, you know, corduroy-jacketed academics.

They are by and large lefty academics who have no real standing in the matter, and I think are highly unlikely to be influential on Britain. This is a very, very small minority in our country who are calling for this."

Without question, many British professors pioneered the academic-animated boycotts targeting Israel. Yet economic body blows to Israel are also emanating from the UK and the Continent. The world's largest security company—the British-based GS4 —announced in March its departure from Israel. BDS rapidly claimed victory.

However, writing in Tablet in late June, Eugene Kontorovich, a law professor at Northwestern University School of Law who specializes in lawfare, said: "It turns out that one of the BDS movement's biggest alleged successes is a colossal failure. Thanks to the new wave of state anti-boycott laws, it has emerged that far from boycotting Israel, the security giant G4S plans to continue doing business there indefinitely."

The Illinois anti-BDS law reversed the G4S boycott of Israel, as Kontorovich wrote: "Illinois sent the company a notice that it might find itself subject to divestment by the state."

Israel announced its opening salvo against BDS, particularly in Europe, to the *Jerusalem Post* in April. Public Security Minister Gilad Erdan said then: "We continue to urge all financial institutions to carefully consider the potential legal, reputational and ethical consequences of facilitating the activities of BDS groups." Since Erdan's shot across the bows of European banks to draw their attention to this issue, five financial institutions spanning France, Austria and Germany have terminated BDS accounts.

All this helps to explain that a multi-layered economic warfare campaign against BDS, which includes political, legal and financial pressure, can influence an astonishingly fast change in corporate behavior.

The questions for counter-terrorist officials and anti-BDS activists to examine are: which radical Islamic organizations and states have infused cash into BDS groups and their activities in Europe? It is worth recalling that Hezbollah's so-called political organization remains legal in Europe (with the exception of the Netherlands). Germany's new federal intelligence report from late June showed 950 Hezbollah members and supporters in the Federal Republic, as well as 300 Hamas members and activists. To better understand BDS and terrorism, the questions that surfaces are, what is the nature of the Hamas and Hezbollah funding sources in Germany? Exhibit A for the interplay between terrorism and BDS was the Austrian-Arab cultural center's event with Leila Khaled, a member of the Popular Front for the Liberation of Palestine, which the US and European Union have designated as a terrorist entity.

Khaled is infamous for her hijackings, which included TWA flight 840 in 1969 and EL AL flight 219 a year later.

The Vienna-based cultural center advocates BDS, and Khaled defended the right to murder Israeli civilians during her April talk. As a result of the terror link, the Austrian bank Bawag shut the center's bank account in June.

Terror finance and its links to BDS is a scarcely researched sector. Take the example of the Iranian regime-sponsored Blue mosque and its Islamic Center in Hamburg.

According to the daily *Hamburger Morgenpost* newspaper, the Iranian- backed institutions played a key role in the pro-BDS al-Quds day march in Berlin. The paper reported that Germany's intelligence agency said approximately 200 people, who regularly attend services at the Blue mosque, participated in the protest calling for the obliteration of Israel. The head of the Islamic Center

Hamburg (IZH) is Reza Ramezani, a loyal disciple of Iran's Supreme Leader Ali Khamenei.

The Hamburg Sparkasse bank provides an account to the IZH. While Germany and most European countries have not developed the sophisticated anti-terror finance operations that exist in the US Treasury department, the Federal Republic is capable of countering BDS funding streams tinged with terrorism. It is a matter of activating political will.

Germany's neighbor France has invoked its 2003 anti-discrimination Lellouche law to squelch BDS campaigns, including the application of robust criminal penalties. In contrast to tough anti-BDS legal measures in the US, France, and in British city councils, German politicians reject penalties with teeth to stop BDS.

The journalist André Anchuelo surveyed German politicians from across the political spectrum in April. Writing in the German Jewish weekly Jüdische Allgemeine, Anchuelo reported that the Left Party MP Petra Pau said a law against Israel boycotts is "disproportionate."

Her colleague MP Jan Korte said a law is "the wrong way" and wants more education. The Social Democrat MP and deputy chairwoman of the German-Israel parliamentary group, Kerstin Griese, considers the current legal situation sufficient.

The Christian Democratic Union MP Gita Connemann said an anti-BDS law would be "difficult" to enact because it might be unconstitutional. Municipal- funded BDS in Germany is prevalent.

The cities of Munich and Bremen, to name just two, allow BDS groups and activists to use city-funded buildings to promote BDS. The Bremen-owned Villa Ichon center furnished the BDS group Bremen Peace Forum with office space.

The group, which urges a boycott of all Israeli goods, marched through Bremen stores in November to seize Israeli products for opprobrium.

In April, the city council of Bayreuth – famous for its annual Richard Wagner opera festival—awarded €10,000 to the pro-BDS group Code Pink for its tolerance work and contributions to humanity. Code Pink immediately announced it would use the prize money to fund a pro-BDS conference in Europe to explain "how false allegations of anti-Semitism have been used to silence this criticism."

Bayreuth is a textbook example for why economic warfare against BDS is in a nascent phase in Germany in particular, and Europe in general. External actors launched no offensive financial warfare against the Bavarian city and its assets in the US. Nearly half of the US states have passed anti-BDS legislation or resolutions.

The key takeaway: The trans-Atlantic relationship will provide a bundle of opportunities to blunt BDS in Europe.

Periodical and Internet Sources Bibliography

The following articles have been selected to supplement the diverse views presented in this chapter.

Naftali Bennett, "My Country Bars Enemies from Entry. Yours Would Do the Same," *New York Times*, January 26, 2018. https://www .nytimes.com/2018/01/26/opinion/israel-bds-entry.html.

Yermi Brenner, "Germany's BDS Movement and the Paradox of Anti-Semitism," Newsgrid, April 21, 2016. https://www.aljazeera.com /indepth/features/2016/04/germany-bds-movement-paradox -anti-semitism-160421084206294.html.

Nada Elia, "The Impact, and Opportunity, of Israel's BDS Ban," *Mondoweiss*, January 11, 2018. http://mondoweiss.net/2018/01 /impact-opportunity-israels.

Government of Canada, "Canadian Policy on Key Issues in the Israeli-Palestinian Conflict," Government of Canada, March 4, 2018. http:// www.international.gc.ca/world-monde/international_relations -relations_internationales/mena-moan/israeli-palistinian_policy -politique_israelo-palestinien.aspx?lang=eng.

Sami Jitan, "Jordan and the Effort to Support BDS in the Arab World," Electronic Intifada, July 20, 2012. https://electronicintifada.net /content/jordan-and-effort-support-bds-arab-world/11516.

Cnaan Liphshiz, "Why Spain Is Standing Up to BDS — For Now," *Times of Israel*, August 15, 2016. https://www.timesofisrael.com /why-spain-is-standing-up-to-bds-for-now.

Raphael Medoff, "Major Jewish Organizations Back Israel's BDS Entry Ban, Barred Group Calls It 'Bullying," *Jewish News Syndicate,* January 17, 2018. https://www.jns.org/major-jewish-organizations -back-israels-bds-entry-ban-barred-group-calls-it-bullying.

Asad Rehman, "BDS Blacklist Is Straight Out Of Apartheid. The UK Can't Condone It," *Guardian*, January 9, 2018.

Jonathan S. Tobin, "I Despise BDS — but Israel's New BDS Ban Is a Big Mistake," Algemeiner, January 12, 2018. https://www .algemeiner.com/2018/01/12/i-despise-bds-but-israels-new-bds -ban-is-a-big-mistake/

CHAPTER 4

Is BDS Anti-Semitic?

Classifying BDS as Anti-Semitic Is a Tactic of Distraction

Yoav Galai

In the following viewpoint, Yoav Galai argues that Israel's prime minister Benjamin Netanyahu is using claims of anti-Semitism to distract from the human rights violations he is committing. The author contends Netanyahu is falsely charging the BDS movement, a reaction to his own policy-driven mistreatment of the Palestinian people, as a movement to destroy the state of Israel. The author implores the reader and others to look beyond the distraction. A former journalist, Galai is a postdoctoral fellow at the department of International Relations at the Central European University. His research focuses on the role narratives of collective memory play in International Relations, both in helping define possibilities for action and as the object of policy.

As you read, consider the following questions:

1. Why did then president Obama say that Netanyahu's stance eroded Israel's credibility?
2. What was the importance of the "FIFA incident" according to the viewpoint?
3. Why does the author say Netanyahu's claims of anti-semitism with regard to boycotting are a "smokescreen"?

I n a recent interview with Israeli television the US president, Barack Obama, warned that the stance adopted by Israel's prime minister, Benjamin Netanyahu, towards the Palestinians erodes Israel's credibility. Preventing the formation of a Palestinian state was Netanyahu's campaign promise and—while he has since backed off—Obama argued that the list of caveats that Netanyahu provided made the chances of any sort of agreement with the Palestinians unlikely.

The fourth Netanyahu government is his most right-wing. Avigdor Lieberman's withdrawal from coalition negotiations at the very last minute inflated the seat-value of the thin majority government and the Likud's partners took advantage of their immense bargaining power to acquire sectarian benefits.

The eight-member Jewish Home Party gained control over the ministries of education and justice – both prestigious portfolios with far-reaching effects on the shape of Israeli society, namely curriculum changes and the restraining of the Supreme Court.

But their gains for the settlement movement are particularly interesting and have the effect of further institutionalising the settlement project. First, the minister of agriculture, settler leader Uri Ariel, gained control over the settlement division in the world Zionist organisation, an amorphous non-governmental body that supports settlement activity in the West Bank.

Second, the Jewish Home was allocated a new post of a deputy security minister with responsibility for the civil administration in the West Bank. Jewish Home leader Naftali Bennett has been pushing Netanyahu to annex Area C in the West Bank (which is already subject to full Israeli civil and security control) and – while there has as yet been no annexation – the creation of this new post gives direct control over that area directly to a Jewish Home representative.

Third, according to the coalition agreements, a special task force is drafting a plan to retroactively legitimise "structures and neighbourhoods in the Jewish Settlements in Judea and Sumaria". Plenty there to raise the ire of the world community.

As Israeli NGO Peace Now demonstrates, the expansion of settlements is ingrained in the coalition agreements that allowed Netanyahu to form the government. As defence minister Moshe Ya'alon stated, expansion has in effect been institutionalised as policy, setting Israel on a collision course with the international community.

But what has emerged from both the bureaucratic chaos and the dire diplomatic prospects is a rather clear stance that is extended from the domestic sphere all the way to the state's foreign policy —anti-boycott.

The Threat of Boycott

Following the FIFA incident, in which the Palestinians withdrew a motion to expel Israel from the organisation, but still subjected it to support a harsh resolution with operational consequences, the threat of boycott has taken tangible form.

It has since become the biggest item on Israel's foreign policy agenda. Here's how Netanyahu articulated the danger:

> We are in the midst of a great struggle being waged against the state of Israel, an international campaign to blacken its name. It is not connected to our actions; it is connected to our very existence. It does not matter what we do; it matters what we symbolise and what we are.

This is nothing new. Netanyahu and other Israeli politicians have in the past lambasted the hypocrisy of world opinion and alluded to the anti-Semitic underpinning of boycott campaigns, but the current level of anxiety in Israel—or rather the level of fanning of anxiety by Israel's politicians and media—is unprecedented.

After being criticised for its anti-Netanyahu stance during the election campaign, *Yedioth*, Israel's second largest daily newspaper, has launched a campaign against boycotts, declaring that it is "mobilising for war, in the form of a series of exposés, articles and reports in the coming weeks and months".

A series of OpEds introduced a repertoire of possible responses to the boycott movement, which, the paper said, was "creating a virtual world" and "following Goebbels." There were separate reports on the dangers of academic and economic boycotts—and even a debate on whether the citizenship of Israeli citizens who support boycott should be revoked. Other media outlets have followed suit.

In fact, the thrust of the anti-boycott campaign has even reached opposition parties—the head of centrist party, Yesh Atid, the journalist Yair Lapid, explained Monday's vote of no confidence, set to topple Netanyahu's government, in terms of the governments' inability to face up to the threat of boycott, writing:

> There is a campaign against the very existence of Israel. Anti-semitic groups, mostly on the left, are leading a campaign that is not against Israeli products. That is not against the settlements. It is against the idea that Jews will have their own state.

At a recent press conference in Canada, Netanyahu lambasted Britain's National Union of Students for its support of the BDS movement:

> Israel has an exemplary democracy. We have academic freedom, press freedom, human rights. ISIS tramples human rights to the dust. It burns people alive in cages and the national student groups in Britain refuse to boycott ISIS and have boycotted Israel. It tells you everything you want to know about the BDS movement.

Meanwhile, in an emergency Knesset debate on the issue the justice minister, Ayelet Shaked, attributed the success of the boycott to "classical antisemitism, radical Islam and naivity," while Ofir Akounis, minister without portfolio, added:

> Perhaps when radical Islam will take over Britain and Europe they will understand the meaning of occupation.

Moral Panic

The BDS campaign, Palestinian appeals to international organisations and denouncements from foreign diplomats no doubt offer challenges to Israel's diplomatic efforts. But lumping such disparate acts together and severing them completely from Israeli actions is an attempt to frame any sort of outside pressure as a priori illegitimate.

If Israeli foreign policy is articulated as merely a response to this pressure, it would leave very little room for diplomacy, let alone open debate—which is already restricted in Israel, where public calls for boycott, even if limited to the West Bank, are already a potentially punishable offence.

The campaign is rather one of moral panic. Boycotters, boycotting and anything that is argued to be within their vicinity are framed as a dangerous existential threat. It is a pre-emptive calibration of public opinion that filters both criticisms from the outside as well as dissenting voices from within.

This well-rehearsed chant being played in the media war-drums does as much to create an atmosphere of crisis as the wailing sirens of the annual emergency drill heard all across Israel. The boycott scare will render any and all criticisms of government policy as part of this existential crisis – which handily enables Netanyahu's government to continue with its projects. For example, it has been reported that a recent purchase of a large church compound in the West Bank through a straw company for the purpose of establishing a new settlement near Hebron will be scrutinised by the civil administration—the responsibility over which is, of course, in the hands of the Jewish Home.

With the government committed to the settlement project, the "look-over-there-ness" of the boycott panic may come in handy.

BDS Is but One Example of a Burgeoning Wave of Anti-Semitism

Steven Horwitz

In the following viewpoint, Steven Horwitz argues that anti-Semitism is on the rise and even equates it to a form of terrorism. The author makes a case that historically, animosity toward the Jewish people has occurred when liberal ideas are under threat. He notes that anti-Semitism can come from both the right and the left and uses the BDS movement as an example of the latter. Horwitz is the Schnatter Distinguished Professor of Free Enterprise in the Department of Economics at Ball State University, where he also is a Fellow at the John H. Schnatter Institute for Entrepreneurship and Free Enterprise. He is the author of Hayek's Modern Family: Classical Liberalism and the Evolution of Social Institutions.

As you read, consider the following questions:

1. According the author, what is the oldest prejudice?
2. What is the root of negative stereotypes of Jews as materialistic and selfish according to the viewpoint?
3. How does the author suggest that economic nationalism can empower anti-Semitism?

Anti-Semitism, it's often said, is the oldest prejudice. The hatred of Jews has waxed and waned over the centuries, but appears to be back with something of a vengeance over the last few years, and especially the last few months.

For example, on Monday, February 27, over two dozen Jewish institutions across the country received bomb threats by anonymous phone calls. These included Jewish Community Centers, synagogues, retirement homes, day care centers, and Jewish educational institutions. These threats are part of a pattern of such threats, including multiple cemetery desecrations, that has been ongoing over the last few months. There have been 100 such threats to Jewish institutions just since the beginning of 2017.

Every time such a threat is called in, these institutions have to clear the building to determine if it is just a hoax. This means rounding up children, infants, the elderly, the infirm, and the developmentally disabled, getting them out of the building and, often, out in the cold, for the hour or two it takes to confirm all is clear. Although, thankfully, these have all turned out to be hoaxes, they still are taking a real toll on the Jewish community and the non-Jews who make use of these institutions. They are, I would argue, a form of terrorism.

The Why of Anti-Semitism

There has been much debate over why these threats have increased in recent months, and it seems plausible that the increased brazenness of the "politically incorrect," including the rise of the alt-right, in the wake of the Trump campaign is probably one key factor. But anti-Semitism is not solely a problem on the Right. The political Left has had its own history of hatred for Jews, manifested in the present by the increased anti-Semitism of the radical Left in the context of criticism of Israel, especially through the Boycott, Divestments, and Sanctions (BDS) movement.

The sources of anti-Semitism on both Right and Left are complicated, but one element on both sides is that Jews have historically been associated with important liberal ideas such as capitalism, entrepreneurship, cosmopolitanism, and free migration. These institutions have enabled massive social, cultural, and economic change, empowering the previously powerless all over the world, and threatening the old order.

The enemies of liberalism have problems with all of these, though the Right and Left differ on which bothers them the most. But for both, Jews can be easily seen as the enemies of those who find deep flaws with the classical liberal social order. When Jews are being threatened, it is usually a good sign that the foundations of liberalism are as well.

Jewish Anti-Capitalism

One point to note up front is that Jews themselves have a history of opposition to classical liberalism. Jewish intellectuals have had a long-standing attraction to socialism, starting of course with Marx himself. In particular, a number of the architects of the Russian Revolution were Jews or of Jewish heritage.

I raise this because I am not arguing that Jews were somehow reliably classically liberal over the last few centuries. And the fact that a good number of Jews were socialist, or that a good number of socialists were Jews, certainly doesn't justify anti-Semitism by critics of socialism.

I do think that part of the attraction of socialism to Jews was its universalist aspiration in the form of the trans-national cosmopolitan vision of classical socialism along with its desire to "heal the world" and its strong ethic of concern for the least well-off. Those aspirations were shared by 19th-century classical liberals and were also part of Jewish practice. This universalism made Jews the target of the critics of classical liberalism from the Right, as well as the right-wing critics of socialism.

Jewish Pro-Capitalism

The association of Jews with capitalism, trade, and entrepreneurship is well known. The negative stereotypes of acquisitiveness, materialism, and selfishness that have long been part of anti-Semitism grew out of the truth that Jews were more likely to be traders and financiers than were other groups. Part of this was that as a nomadic people, Jews invested in their human capital rather than the physical capital they would have had to schlep around while getting kicked out of country after country.

(This might also explain why Jews have also been disproportionately entertainers and intellectuals. The skills for telling jokes, writing stories, making music, or working in the realm of ideas are ones that don't require much in the way of physical capital in order to be successful.)

Jews were also often middlemen as a result of their nomadic existence and familiarity with so many parts of the world. Middlemen have always been suspect to the economically ignorant as far back as Aristotle, as they appear to profit by creating nothing tangible. This is particularly true when the middlemen are in financial markets, where they are not even trading something physical.

It's no surprise, therefore, that hatred of capitalism has been accompanied by hatred of the Jews.

Right-wing anti-Semitism, however, often draws upon these capitalist tropes as part of its hatred. But in this context, Jews are not so much seen as representative of capitalist exploitation that can be ended by socialism, but rather as an example of people who place love of money and their universalist aspirations above the love of their country and its citizens.

German anti-Semitism in the 20th century had roots in the argument that Jews had been "war profiteers" in World War I and had benefitted from the economic destruction that characterized the Weimar Republic period leading up to Hitler's ascension to power. The Nazis, and other fascist movements, saw the Jews as the sort of rootless cosmopolitans who were unable to grasp the importance of blood and soil.

The modern version of this point, and one that is also found on the Left, is the "dual loyalty" charge laid upon pro-Israel Jews: they are beholden to Israel in ways that cause them to work against the interests of the United States.

The Why of Nationalism

One way to see the "national socialism" of various fascist movements is that they objected not to socialism per se, but to socialism's attempt to put class ahead of race or ethnicity or nationality. To the fascists, German or Italian workers shared much more with German or Italian capitalists than they did with Russian or American workers. Marxian socialism drew the wrong battle lines.

And so it is today, as "economic nationalism" is on the rise globally and Jews have again become the most obvious target for an invigorated Right. Jews have always been the symbol of the cosmopolitan, the migrant, and the "rootless" trader. If you reject market-driven globalization, whether because you dislike markets or because you are a nationalist, you are going to have reasons to see Jews as symbols of what you reject. That opposition to immigration and global trade, and the market system that is at the root of both, would go hand-in-hand with anti-Semitism is hardly surprising.

The economic nationalism of Trump and a variety of European leaders is not inherently anti-Semitic, nor does it require that the leaders of such movements be anti-Semites, but the arguments of economic nationalism can easily empower the anti-Semitism of both the Right and Left. The leaders build in plausible deniability, knowing full well the nature of the forces they are unleashing but in ways that avoid direct responsibility.

How could they not know? We have centuries of experience to draw on, back to the ancient world through the Middle Ages all the way to the ghastly slaughter of the 20th century during which anti-Semitism nearly destroyed the whole of Europe itself. The costs have been unspeakable, and hence the vow to never forget. And yet, despite this history, the tendency to forget remains. To remember would require that we think more clearly about ideology and philosophy, human rights and dignity. Many people do not want to do that. It remains easier to scapegoat than to remember.

Admittedly, we liberals have a special grudge against anti-Semitism. It broke up the greatest intellectual society of the

20th century, shattering Viennese intellectual life, flinging even Ludwig von Mises out of his home and into the abyss. His books were banned, and those of many others too. He and so many fled for their lives but bravely rebuilt them in the new world that offered protection.

A Warning Sign

It has been said that Jews are the canaries in the coal mine of a liberal society: when they are under threat, it is a warning sign. The ongoing and increasing threats to Jewish communities here in the US, as well as similar trends across Europe, should have all of us worried. A world where Jews sing out in joy together and are unafraid to fly free is one far more safe from tyranny than one in which we Jews worry about dying in our own cages, as many of us are doing as the threats to our institutions have become more frequent and more brazen in recent months.

Watch how a society treats Jews and you'll have an indicator of its degree of openness and respect for liberty. When Jews are being threatened, so are the deepest of our liberal values. The poisonous air from coal mining that killed canaries was invisible. The threats to Jews and to liberalism are not. Citizens of liberal societies dismiss or downplay those threats at our own peril.

Not Every Criticism of Israel Is Anti-Semitic

Iain Banks

In the following viewpoint, Iain Banks argues that he supports the BDS movement because he "can." As a writer, Banks feels that he can make a difference. He cites how the sporting boycott of South Africa helped end apartheid because the South Africans valued cricket and rugby so much. Similarly, he feels that an intellectual boycott of Israel can have much power. Banks believes that "constructive engagement and reasoned argument" have not worked in bringing Israel to change its ways and that a boycott is all that's left. For too long the world has turned its back on Palestinian suffering. It is time to act. Banks is a Scottish author. He has written dozens of books including The Wasp Factory *and the nine-book Culture series of science fiction novels. He is the recipient of numerous awards.*

As you read, consider the following questions:

1. What action against South Africa does the author compare the BDS campaign?
2. What does the author claim is the "particular tragedy" of Israel's treatment of Palestinians?
3. Why does the author write that we are punishing ourselves when we punish others?

"Iain Banks: Why I'm Supporting a Cultural Boycott of Israel," by Iain M Banks, Guardian News and Media Limited, April 5, 2015. Reprinted by permission.

I support the Boycott, Divestment and Sanctions (BDS) campaign because, especially in our instantly connected world, an injustice committed against one, or against one group of people, is an injustice against all, against every one of us; a collective injury.

My particular reason for participating in the cultural boycott of Israel is that, first of all, I can; I'm a writer, a novelist, and I produce works that are, as a rule, presented to the international market. This gives me a small extra degree of power over that which I possess as a (UK) citizen and a consumer. Secondly, where possible when trying to make a point, one ought to be precise, and hit where it hurts. The sports boycott of South Africa when it was still run by the racist apartheid regime helped to bring the country to its senses because the ruling Afrikaaner minority put so much store in their sporting prowess. Rugby and cricket in particular mattered to them profoundly, and their teams' generally elevated position in the international league tables was a matter of considerable pride. When they were eventually isolated by the sporting boycott—as part of the wider cultural and trade boycott —they were forced that much more persuasively to confront their own outlaw status in the world.

A sporting boycott of Israel would make relatively little difference to the self-esteem of Israelis in comparison to South Africa; an intellectual and cultural one might help make all the difference, especially now that the events of the Arab spring and the continuing repercussions of the attack on the Gaza-bound flotilla peace convoy have threatened both Israel's ability to rely on Egypt's collusion in the containment of Gaza, and Turkey's willingness to engage sympathetically with the Israeli regime at all. Feeling increasingly isolated, Israel is all the more vulnerable to further evidence that it, in turn, like the racist South African regime it once supported and collaborated with, is increasingly regarded as an outlaw state.

I was able to play a tiny part in South Africa's cultural boycott, ensuring that—once it thundered through to me that I could do so—my novels weren't sold there (while subject to an earlier contract, under whose terms the books were sold in South Africa, I did a rough calculation of royalties earned each year and sent that amount to the ANC). Since the 2010 attack on the Turkish-led convoy to Gaza in international waters, I've instructed my agent not to sell the rights to my novels to Israeli publishers. I don't buy Israeli-sourced products or food, and my partner and I try to support Palestinian-sourced products wherever possible.

It doesn't feel like much, and I'm not completely happy doing even this; it can sometimes feel like taking part in collective punishment (although BDS is, by definition, aimed directly at the state and not the people), and that's one of the most damning charges that can be levelled at Israel itself: that it engages in the collective punishment of the Palestinian people within Israel, and the occupied territories, that is, the West Bank and – especially – the vast prison camp that is Gaza. The problem is that constructive engagement and reasoned argument demonstrably have not worked, and the relatively crude weapon of boycott is pretty much all that's left. (To the question, "What about boycotting Saudi Arabia?"—all I can claim is that cutting back on my consumption of its most lucrative export was a peripheral reason for giving up the powerful cars I used to drive, and for stopping flying, some years ago. I certainly wouldn't let a book of mine be published there either, although—unsurprisingly, given some of the things I've said about that barbaric excuse for a country, not to mention the contents of the books themselves – the issue has never arisen, and never will with anything remotely resembling the current regime in power.)

As someone who has always respected and admired the achievements of the Jewish people – they've probably contributed even more to world civilisation than the Scots, and we Caledonians are hardly shy about promoting our own wee-but-influential record and status—and has felt sympathy for the suffering they experienced, especially in the years leading up to and then during the second world war and the Holocaust, I'll always feel uncomfortable taking part in any action that—even if only thanks to the efforts of the Israeli propaganda machine—may be claimed by some to target them, despite the fact that the state of Israel and the Jewish people are not synonymous. Israel and its apologists can't have it both ways, though: if they're going to make the rather hysterical claim that any and every criticism of Israeli domestic or foreign policy amounts to antisemitism, they have to accept that this claimed, if specious, indivisibility provides an opportunity for what they claim to be the censure of one to function as the condemnation of the other.

The particular tragedy of Israel's treatment of the Palestinian people is that nobody seems to have learned anything. Israel itself was brought into being partly as a belated and guilty attempt by the world community to help compensate for its complicity in, or at least its inability to prevent, the catastrophic crime of the Holocaust. Of all people, the Jewish people ought to know how it feels to be persecuted en masse, to be punished collectively and to be treated as less than human. For the Israeli state and the collective of often unlikely bedfellows who support it so unquestioningly throughout the world to pursue and support the inhumane treatment of the Palestinian people—forced so brutally off their land in 1948 and still under attack today—to be so blind to the idea that injustice is injustice, regardless not just on whom it is visited, but by whom as well, is one of the defining iniquities of our age, and powerfully implies a shamingly low upper limit on the extent of our species' moral intelligence.

The solution to the dispossession and persecution of one people can never be to dispossess and persecute another. When we do this, or participate in this, or even just allow this to happen without criticism or resistance, we only help ensure further injustice, oppression, intolerance, cruelty and violence in the future.

We may see ourselves as many tribes, but we are one species, and in failing to speak out against injustices inflicted on some of our number and doing what we can to combat those without piling further wrongs on earlier ones, we are effectively collectively punishing ourselves.

The BDS campaign for justice for the Palestinian people is one I would hope any decent, open-minded person would support. Gentile or Jew, conservative or leftist, no matter who you are or how you see yourself, these people are our people, and collectively we have turned our backs on their suffering for far too long.

Ignoring Islamic Anti-Semitism Is Dangerous

Haviv Rettig Gur

In the following viewpoint, Haviv Rettig Gur reminds readers that anti-Semitism is not only a historical hatred, but a current one. He quotes hate speech by two current world leaders to demonstrate that anti-Semitism is alive and well worldwide. Such ideology poses a danger on a global level. When one social movement demonizes another, history tells us that catastrophe will follow. But it is fashionable now on college campuses to support Islamic causes and ignore the underlying hatred of Jews. Critiques of the Arab-Israeli conflict have their place, but it is well to critique the critiques and raise awareness that some of the left leaning academics are supporting ideologies that publicly call for civilian murder. Rettig Gur is an Israeli journalist who serves as the political correspondent and analyst for The Times of Israel. *He was born in Jerusalem to American-born parents and formerly worked for the* Jerusalem Post.

As you read, consider the following questions:

1. How does the author remind the reader that anti-Semitism is alive and well?
2. Why do most studies of anti-Semitism focus on history and not on current events?
3. What is problematic about intellectual left-wing's support of Islamic causes?

The Europeans killed six million Jews out of 12 million. But today the Jews rule this world by proxy. They get others to fight and die for them. They invented socialism, communism, human rights, and democracy so that persecuting them would appear to be wrong, so they may enjoy equal rights with others. With these [inventions], they have now gained control of the most powerful countries. And they, this tiny community, have become a world power."

Those words, as clear an expression of classical anti-Semitic tropes as one could hope to find, were not uttered by white supremacists in an American prison or in a Bin Laden video broadcast from the mountains of the Hindu Kush.

Neither was this quote: "Dear brothers, we must not forget to nurse our children and grandchildren on hatred towards those Zionists and Jews, and all those who support them. They must be nursed on hatred. The hatred must continue."

Those who follow the anti-Semitic utterances of Muslim leaders will recognize both diatribes.

The first was uttered in 2003 by Mahathir Mohamad, Malaysia's longest-serving prime minister. Mohamad was not caught unawares by the camera. He was not embarrassed when his words were broadcast. In fact, his warnings about Jewish power and the nefarious Jewish invention of both communism and democracy were delivered from a broad, wood-paneled stage before hundreds of heads of state and ambassadors from 116 countries gathered at the Organization of the Islamic Conference summit in Kuala Lumpur.

As head of state of the host nation, it was his moment in the sun. And in a sweeping speech on world affairs, he made sure to warn the world about the power of the Jews.

The second quote was delivered more recently—and closer to home. It was uttered by none other than Egypt's current president, Mohammed Morsi, the leader of Israel's largest neighbor, just two years ago.

The world knows all about these views, which are voiced daily in media outlets throughout the Muslim world, and often make their way into the speeches of Muslim heads of state. But the world shrugs.

And that, according to sociologist Dr. Charles Small, does not bode well for the future of the Muslim world—or for the rest of us.

"There is a crisis in the world," says Small, an Oxford-educated Canadian-Israeli scholar of anti-Semitism, in a recent conversation with the *Times of Israel.*

The danger does not come from Islam itself, he emphasizes. The Muslim world is as big and complex as any great civilization.

Rather, "we're talking about all the variations of radical political Islam, or Islamism, which is a term I prefer to use." Islamism, a modern political ideology that seeks to borrow legitimacy from Islamic text and tradition, "has at its ideological core a profoundly deadly anti-Semitism. Al-Qaeda certainly has it. And Morsi's Muslim Brotherhood have had it since their inception, for nearly a century," Small says.

Iran's rulers have it, too. Indeed, it has seeped into the mainstream of political discourse in countless Muslims societies.

The danger to the world should be obvious. "When a social movement demonizes the other, we know from history this will be a catastrophe. It's already a moral and ethical catastrophe, and it's going to be a political catastrophe. It's only a matter of time before others will be painted with the same brush. If we've learned anything from history, we've learned this."

Whither go the Jews, there other minorities and freedoms will follow.

But hasn't it all been said before, one immediately wonders. The answer, Small insists, is no.

"I think there was this belief or hope that anti-Semitism died in Auschwitz, that anti-Semitism miraculously disappeared after the Holocaust."

That naivete has meant a surprising scarcity of academic interest in contemporary anti-Semitism.

"It's striking. Every research center on anti-Semitism in the world, including in Israel, is run by historians, and it's not focused on contemporary issues. The fact that our group at Yale was the first research center [on anti-Semitism] in an American university—is itself a research question. Why did it take until 2006 for this to happen?"

YIISA, the Yale Institute for the Interdisciplinary Study of Antisemitism, was established in 2006 by the nonprofit Institute for the Study of Global Antisemitism and Policy (ISGAP) which Small heads. The Yale institute produced research papers and conferences, including in 2011 the largest-ever academic conference on anti-Semitism.

YIISA was closed by the university under mysterious circumstances in 2011. A report by the university review board that recommended shutting the institute was declared confidential and has not been made public. Review panel member Donald Green, head of the university's Institution for Social and Policy Studies, YIISA's umbrella body at the university, said the institute "failed to meet high standards for research and instruction."

The institute had drawn fire from campus organizations, the PLO ambassador, and numerous anti-Israel blogs for engaging in "advocacy," with a few accusing the institute of open Islamophobia and anti-Arab prejudice.

But the closure drew a torrent of criticism. Walter Reich, former director of the US Holocaust Memorial Museum and a professor at George Washington University who was on YIISA's academic board of advisers, lamented in the *Washington Post* that "Yale just killed the country's best institute for the study of anti-Semitism."

He called the closure "strange," praised the institute's "quality and output" as "superb and wide-ranging," and explained Yale's decision as political.

At the 2011 conference, he wrote, "Some [invited scholars] spoke, inevitably, about the fastest-growing and most virulent manifestation of contemporary anti-Semitism—the anti-Semitism in the Arab/Muslim world, in which the tropes of classic European anti-Semitism (such as the allegations that Jews meet secretly to control the world, murder non-Jewish children to use their blood

Left-Wing Hypocricies?

In an essay that's likely to raise some eyebrows on the left—and be cheered by the right—Jay Michaelson, a prominent American Jewish progressive voice and gay activist who writes a column for the Forward, comes down hard on the Jewish left wing for its hypocrisies when it comes to Israel. He writes:

> …my aim in this column is to call out my liberal colleagues on certain of our blind spots and try to communicate to fellow progressives when, in my view, their criticism of Israel becomes deeply problematic — even, dare I say it, anti-Semitic. I do so because, just as I am uncomfortable in Jewish nationalist circles where people routinely make racist, violent and ethnocentric remarks (and where those remarks support real-world policies with real effects on real people), so, too, I am uncomfortable in left-wing circles where some people evince a casual disregard for the legitimate concerns of Israelis and Jews, for the very real and very deep problems on the Palestinian side, and even for the truth.

Michaelson offers four main criticisms:

1. "There is a problematic lack of disclosure among many critics of Israel that their ultimate view is that Israel should not exist at all." Exhibit A: Jewish Voice for Peace, many of whose members favor ending the Jewish state.

2. Why do proponents of a one-state solution (read "selective cultural genocide") favor that scenario only for Israel, but not elsewhere in the world where there are conflicts between majorities and minorities? "This is where anti-Zionism slides into anti-Semitism," Michaelson writes.

3. By focusing inordinately on Israel and ignoring human rights abuses elsewhere, the left absurdly has Israel "depicted as the most oppressive country on Earth."

4. The left defines Israel solely by its occupation and ignores other aspects of its multifaceted society, while the Palestinians get a free pass on everything from human rights abuses to treatment of gays.

"Jay Michaelson Slams the left on Israel," by Uriel Heilman, Jewish Telegraphic Agency, July 30, 2012.

in Jewish rituals and spread disease to kill non-Jews) have been not only adopted but also embellished.

"To be sure," Reich continued, "some presenters expressed alarm and took an activist stance—as do some presenters at academic conferences on genocide, human rights, women's studies, African American studies, Hispanic studies, gay and lesbian studies, and nuclear proliferation."

Harvard law professor Alan Dershowitz complained that the closure was conducted "without even a semblance of due process and transparency," with the review panel's report kept confidential even from Small himself.

Whatever problems Yale may have found, said the ADL's Abe Foxman, "what was required was a concerted effort to work out the problems rather than ending the program. Especially at a time when anti-Semitism continues to be virulent and anti-Israel parties treat any effort to address issues relating to anti-Zionism and anti-Semitism as illegitimate, Yale's decision is particularly unfortunate and dismaying."

Small's supporters believe it was the very attempt to deal with contemporary anti-Semitism, especially in the societies where it is most widespread and least challenged, that doomed America's first institute of its kind.

For Small, the Yale experience, cut off so suddenly after six years, is a signal that his work is hitting a nerve and challenging a real problem.

"There's a reluctance among scholars to open up this subject," he says in his polite, affable way. "This subject is dangerous, embarrassing. It touches on various political interests in international relations that people don't really want to engage with."

Engaging with that issue is what ISGAP is all about. Now freed of its Yale anchor, ISGAP has begun to grow.

Over the past year, it has run ongoing seminar lectures at Harvard Law School, Stanford, McGill and Fordham universities. From its base in a small office in Midtown Manhattan—the institute is run on a shoestring budget, with a coordinator on each campus and a small handful of administrative staff in New York—ISGAP has turned its attention to commissioning new research projects. A book of papers will be published in the spring and conferences are planned for next year.

Its modest goal: "To understand anti-Semitism.

"We need to be interdisciplinary and critical. We need people on the ground, who speak Arabic and Farsi, to understand the history and sociology and anthropology" of the societies being studied.

The institute plans to study academia, too. "We need an intellectual approach, to understand philosophically why radical Islam has such acquiescence, how the West aids and abets a social movement such as the Muslim Brotherhood that is [so radically opposed to its values]." Part of that question must deal with the culture in Western academia, says Small. "You have the politically correct element on American campuses, where people believe that if you start examining anti-Semitism in the Middle East, you're making excuses for Israel. You have people like [renowned feminist philosopher] Judith Butler, a brilliant woman, gay, Jewish, a serious intellectual, who can get up and argue that Hamas and Hezbollah, because they are anti-Zionist, are part of the progressive movement."

Butler, who has supported some of the boycott efforts directed at Israel, was criticized last summer for suggesting Hamas and Hezbollah should be understood as "social movements that are progressive, that are on the left, that are part of a global left." She has said she opposes violence, that placing such organization on the "left" does not necessarily imply support for them, and that she has "never taken a stand on either organization."

But for Small, that sort of discourse, where a liberal progressive intellectual can refuse to take a stance on supporting or critiquing radical religious organizations that publicly call for the murder of civilian populations, shows that there is something missing from the debate in academia.

"The post-modern critique has some truth and some insights," he says. "But we also have to critique the critique. We have to get young brilliant scholars to get into the battle of ideas and have a sophisticated analysis of today's canon and how it affects the rights of Jews around the world, and gay people, and minorities. Are we equipped in a sophisticated manner to understand the rise of political Islam around the world and critique it? Until we have an interdisciplinary, critical analysis of what's going on, we won't have any answers, just descriptions of unfortunate situations. As scholars we have a moral obligation to help create policies that will promote human rights and dignity for all. We cannot allow the attempts to silence to prevail—the human cost is just too high."

BDS Is a Principled Response to Israel's Actions

Donna Nevel

In the following viewpoint, Donna Nevel writes that while many American Jews support civil and human rights, they abandon their principles when it comes to BDS, claiming the campaign is anti-Semitic. She cites a Palestine Liberation Organization (PLO) member who states that the movement does not target Jews, and rejects anti-Semitism. Rather than engage in productive debate with BDS supporters, those against BDS resort to mischaracterization, name calling, and economic attacks. But it is not BDS that Jews should oppose, but the practices of the Israeli government that made BDS necessary. Nevel, a community psychologist and educator, is codirector of PARCEO, a participatory research center. She is a long-time organizer against islamophobia and anti-Arab racism, for justice in Palestine, and for justice in public education. She is cofounder of Jews Against Anti-Muslim Racism and is on the coordinating committee of Facing the Nakba.

As you read, consider the following questions:

1. Why have many Jews abandoned their core principles when it comes to BDS?
2. How do the stated goals of BDS clash with its characterization as an anti-Semitic movement?
3. How should anti-BDS factions respond to the situation going forward?

"Boycott, Divestment, and Sanctions (BDS) and the American Jewish Community," by Donna Nevel, Tikkun Daily, March 7, 2014. Reprinted by permission.

Many American Jewish organizations claim to be staunch supporters of civil and human rights as well as academic freedom. But when it comes to Boycott, Divestment, and Sanctions (BDS) against Israel, they make an exception. In their relentless opposition to BDS, they leave even core principles behind.

The Palestinian-led call for BDS, which began in 2005 in response to ongoing Israeli government violations of basic principles of international law and human rights of the Palestinian people, is a call of conscience. It has strengthened markedly over the last few years among artists, students, unions, church groups, dockworkers, and others. Media coverage of endorsers of the boycott has gone mainstream and viral. Recent examples include Stephen Hawking's refusal to go to Jerusalem for the Presidential Conference, the successful campaign surrounding Scarlett Johansson's support for Soda Stream and its settlement operation, and the American Studies Association (ASA) resolution that endorsed boycott of Israeli academic institutions.

Alongside BDS's increasing strength have come increasingly virulent attacks on, and campaigns against it. These attacks tend to employ similar language and tactics—as if the groups are all cribbing from the same talking points—including tarring BDS supporters as "anti-Semitic" and "delegitimizers."

These attacks simply don't address or grapple with the core aspirations or realities of BDS. As described by Hanan Ashrawi, executive committee member of the PLO, in a recent letter in the *New York Times*, BDS "does not target Jews, individually or collectively, and rejects all forms of bigotry and discrimination, including anti-Semitism." She goes on to explain that "B.D.S. is, in fact, a legal, moral and inclusive movement struggling against the discriminatory policies of a country that defines itself in religiously exclusive terms, and that seeks to deny Palestinians the most basic rights simply because we are not Jewish."

The use of name-calling like "anti-Semites" and "delegitimizers" is problematic for a number of reasons, not only because its claims are untrue, but also because it takes the focus off the real issue at hand—whether and how Israel is, in fact, violating international law and basic human rights principles—and, instead, recklessly impugns the characters of those advocating for Israel to be held accountable.

Criticisms, even extremely harsh ones, of the Israeli state or calls to make a state democratic and adhere to equal rights for all its citizens are not anti-Semitic. Rather, anti-Semitism is about hatred of, and discrimination against the Jewish people, which is not anywhere to be found in the call for BDS, and these kinds of accusations also serve to trivialize the long and ugly history of anti-Semitism.

Most recently, the anti-BDS effort has moved to the legislative front. A bill, introduced in the New York State Assembly last month, would have trampled academic freedom and the right to support BDS in its quest to punish the ASA and deter any who might dare to emulate its endorsement of the academic boycott. Those supporting the bill were opposed by a broad coalition of education, civil rights, legal, academic, and Palestine solidarity organizations, as well as Jewish social justice groups. The bill was withdrawn, but a revised version has been introduced that is designed, like the original, to punish colleges that use public funds for activities related to groups that support boycotts of Israel, including mere attendance at their meetings.

The Jewish Community Relations Council (JCRC) worked closely with the sponsors of the New York bill.

Like the JCRC, rather than engaging in substantive debate about the issues raised in relation to BDS, the Israeli government and many Jewish communal organizations choose, instead, to try to discredit and derail the efforts of those supporting BDS.

For example, as recently reported by Ha'aretz, the Israeli Knesset is debating how to continue to counter BDS efforts across the globe, that is, "whether to launch an aggressive public campaign or operate through quieter, diplomatic channels." It is also considering what the role of AIPAC might be in introducing anti-boycott legislation and how to best bolster military surveillance—which has significant funding behind it–against supporters of BDS.

American Jewish communal organizations have also expended massive resources and energy in their campaigns to demonize endorsers of BDS. The Israel Action Network (IAN)–which describes itself as "a strategic initiative of The Jewish Federations of North America, in partnership with the Jewish Council for Public Affairs (JCPA), created to counter assaults made on Israel's legitimacy"—has funded the anti-BDS effort to the tune of at least six million dollars over a three-year period.

The IAN website characterizes supporters of BDS as "delegitimizers"and says that, in order to gain support from "vulnerable targets," which include "college campuses, churches, labor unions, and human rights organizations," delegitimizers utilize Boycott, Divestment and Sanctions (BDS) tactics, "the same tools used to isolate and vilify apartheid South Africa, Iran, or Nazi Germany. BDS activists, IAN continues, "present distortions, fabrications and misrepresentations of international law in an attempt to paint Israel with the same brush."

In another example of name-calling without any substance, the Anti-Defamation League's (ADL's) July 2013 report attacked Jewish Voice for Peace (JVP), featuring ad hominem accusations (JVP "intentionally exploits Jewish culture"), rather than discussing JVP's actual positions. (A JVP report on the ADL points out that the ADL not only targets JVP but is well-known for its long history of spying on Arabs and supporters of the Palestinian movement.)

On the charge of anti-Semitism, the Simon Wiesenthal Center, in its call to fight the BDS movement, urges it supporters to "learn the facts behind this hypocritical and anti-Semitic campaign," and the ADL's Abe Foxman echoed those same sentiments: "The BDS movement at its very core is anti-Semitic." And most recently, in his speech to AIPAC, Prime Minister Netanyahu, after shamelessly drawing upon classic anti-Semitic imagery of Jews to speak of supporters of BDS, says: "So you see, attempts to boycott, divest and sanction Israel, the most threatened democracy on earth, are simply the latest chapter in the long and dark history of anti-Semitism."

The demonization of BDS is not only the domain of the Israeli government and the mainstream Jewish community. The self-declared liberal J-Street, in its seemingly relentless quest to stay under the Jewish "tent," has also jumped on the anti-BDS bandwagon, sometimes in partnership with the IAN, which (precisely because J Street is positioned as a peace group) proudly documents its relationship with J Street in fighting BDS. Discussing how J Street is gaining acceptance in the mainstream Jewish community, JCPA's CEO Rabbi Steve Gutow points to "its role in pushing back against the boycott, divestment and sanctions movement..."

Further, the refusal of both liberal land mainstream Jewish groups to discuss substantive issues around Israel's actions or BDS also reveals itself in language that admonishes BDS as being "beyond the pale." Recently, for example, as reported by the director of JVP in an op-ed in the Forward, the director of the JCRC of Greater Boston, who has a history of involvement in liberal organizations, explained that "any organization that supports BDS ... doesn't belong at the communal table. In fact, he was referring specifically to Jewish Voice for Peace. He even argued that opening the public conversation to BDS is roughly akin to welcoming the Ku Klux Klan."

This attempted silencing of those simply discussing BDS plays out even in seemingly minor local skirmishes. For example, last year, the liberal rabbi of a large New York City synagogue cancelled the synagogue's facilities-usage contract with a group of Jews who, he feared, might, on his premises, discuss BDS. That, he said, would be "beyond the pale."

These attacks against BDS appear to be an almost desperate reaction to the increasing successes of BDS, not only in the world at large, but also within the broader Jewish community itself. Respected members of the liberal Jewish community as well as a few liberal Zionist groups that were vehemently anti-BDS are now calling for boycotts against products made in the settlements and are engaging with the issue publicly. Further, the mission and vision of groups like Jews Say No and Jewish Voice for Peace —"a diverse and democratic community of activists inspired by Jewish tradition to work together for peace, social justice, and human rights"—are resonating with increasing numbers of Jews who support BDS as a natural outgrowth of their commitments. And that movement is growing in partnership with the broader Palestinian-led movement for justice.

How should the rest of the Jewish community respond? Ad hominem attacks on BDS just will not do. It is time for BDS opponents to take a deep breath. Consider this: BDS is a principled response to Israel's actions and behavior as an occupier. It is a profound call by Palestinians—and supporters world-wide—for justice. It is not BDS that should be opposed, but, rather, the very policies and practices that have made BDS necessary.

Periodical and Internet Sources Bibliography

The following articles have been selected to supplement the diverse views presented in this chapter.

Anti-Defamation League, "BDS: The Global Campaign to Delegitimize Israel," https://www.adl.org/resources /backgrounders/bds-the-global-campaign-to-delegitimize-israel.

Allan C. Brownfeld, "Anti-Zionism Is Not Anti-Semitism, and Never Was," Americans for Middle East Understanding, November 29, 2017. http://www.ameu.org/Current-Issue/Current-Issue/2017 -Volume-50/Anti-Zionism-Is-Not-Anti-Semitism,-And-Never-Was .aspx.

Na'ama Carlin, "Are Israel Boycotts Really Anti-Semitic?" Eureka Street, February 13, 2018. https://www.eurekastreet.com.au /article.aspx?aeid=54664.

Michael Coren, "Why Tossing Around the 'Anti-Semitic' Label Is So Dangerous," iPolitics, January 2, 2018. https://ipolitics .ca/2018/01/02/tossing-around-anti-semitic-label-dangerous.

Graeme Hamilton, "Vote Targeting Jewish Student Politician Was Not Anti-Semitic: McGill report," *National Post*, February 8, 2018. http://nationalpost.com/news/canada/vote-targeting-jewish -student-politician-was-political-not-anti-semitic-mcgill-report.

David Hirsh, "Boycott, Divestment, and Sanctions (BDS) and Antisemitism," Academic Engagement, December, 2016. http:// academicengagement.org/wp-content/uploads/2017/03/David -Hirsh-pamphlet.pdf.

Petra Marquardt-Bigman, "BDS's Roots Are Steeped in Anti-Semitism," Forward, January 9 2018. https://forward.com /opinion/391736/bdss-roots-are-steeped-in-anti-semitism.

David Rosenberg, "BDS Is a Lot of Things, but It's Not Anti-Semitic," *Haaretz*, May 7, 2018. https://www.haaretz.com/opinion/bds-is -a-lot-of-things-but-it-s-not-anti-semitic-1.5440228.

For Further Discussion

Chapter 1
1. After reading about the history of the Palestinian-Israeli dispute, does either side have the moral high ground? Or are there enough wrongs on both sides to place blame equally?
2. Is the Palestinian-Israeli dispute primarily one over land? Is the religious/ethnic/cultural component also a major source of controversy?

Chapter 2
1. After reading the various viewpoints in this chapter, do you think the Boycott, Divest, and Sanction movement seems to be working, or is it a failure? Or, is the reality somewhere in between?
2. Given the history of the Palestinian-Israeli controversy, is the BDS movement justified?

Chapter 3
1. Why are the governments of so many countries opposed to the BDS movement? Why have they largely not sided with the aggrieved Palestinians.
2. What do you think of the legitimacy of the cultural boycott of Israel, which attempts to prevent bands (such as Radiohead) and actors from performing in Israel?
3. Are supporters of BDS divided on ideological grounds? Is the right pro-Israel and the left pro-boycott? Are there those in the middle?

Chapter 4
1. After reading the viewpoints in this chapter, do you believe that BDS is anti-Semitic?
2. Does BDS pose an existential threat to the state of Israel, or is it just a means to create a more diverse Arab-Israeli society?

Organizations to Contact

The editors have compiled the following list of organizations concerned with the issues debated in this book. The descriptions are derived from materials provided by the organizations. All have publications or information available for interested readers. The list was compiled on the date of publication of the present volume; the information provided here may change. Be aware that many organizations take several weeks or longer to respond to inquiries, so allow as much time as possible.

Al Mezan Center for Human Rights
P.O. Box 5270
5/102-Al Mena, Omar El-Mukhtar Street
Gaza City, Gaza Strip, Palestine
+972 (0)8282-0447
email: info@mezan.org
website: www.mezan.org

Al Mezan Center for Human Rights is an independent, nonpartisan, nongovernmental human rights organization based in the Gaza Strip. Established in 1999, Al Mezan has been dedicated to protecting and advancing respect for human rights—especially economic, social and cultural rights—supporting victims of violations of international human rights law and international humanitarian law, and enhancing democracy, community, and citizen participation, and respect for the rule of law in Gaza. Al Mezan's mission is to promote the respect and protection of human rights in the Gaza Strip as part of the occupied Palestinian territory, through research, legal intervention, advocacy, and awareness-raising. They conduct their work by combining of professionalism and community participation. Their guiding principles include equal human worth and equal respect of all human rights, individual and collective, for all people as enshrined in international law and jurisprudence. Their website contains a host of resources for study of the Palestinian-Israeli situation, including press releases, news briefs, position papers, and more.

American Israel Public Affairs Committee (AIPAC)
251 H Street NW
Washington D.C. 2001
(202) 639-5200
email: information@aipaccom
website: www.aipac.com

AIPAC is a pro-Israel advocacy group that was founded in 1963. Their mission is to "strengthen, protect and promote the US-Israel relationship in ways that enhance the security of the United States and Israel." AIPAC's staff and citizen activists attempt to educate decision makers on what unites the United States and Israel and how it is in America's best interest to help keep the Jewish state is safe, strong, and secure. AIPAC believes that cooperation between the two countries is advantageous for both nations. As America's bipartisan pro-Israel lobby, AIPAC "urges all members of Congress to support Israel through foreign aid, government partnerships, joint anti-terrorism efforts, and the promotion of a negotiated two-state solution—a Jewish state of Israel and a demilitarized Palestinian state." The AIPAC website contains numerous resources, including publications, maps, videos, and fact sheets pertaining to Israeli and Israeli-Palestinian issues.

American Task Force on Palestine (ATFP)
1634 Eye Street NW, Suite 725
Washington D.C. 20006
email: info@atfp.net
website: www.americantaskforce.org

The American Task Force on Palestine is a nonprofit, nonpartisan organization that attempts to strengthen American-Palestinian relations. The ATFP attempts to "articulate and educate about the United States national interest in helping to create a Palestinian state living alongside Israel in peace, security, and dignity." The ATFP advocates for diplomacy and legislative efforts. The website includes breaking news, information on recent campaigns, press releases, position papers, commentary, and videos, all concerning the ongoing conflict between Israel and the Palestinians.

Anti-Defamation League (ADL)
605 Third Avenue
New York, NY 10158-3560
(212) 885-7700
website: www.adl.org

Founded in 1913, the ADL is comprised of activists, educators, and experts. They fight anti-Semitism and all forms of hate. The Anti-Defamation League advocates for a safe and secure democratic Jewish State of Israel and combats efforts to delegitimize it. They help shape laws locally and nationally, and develop legislation. The ADL works with students to respect inclusion and to challenge bias and bullying. They train law enforcement officers about extremism, terrorism, and hate crimes. The ADL website contains everything from lesson plans to a resource library containing such materials as a hate symbol database. Their articles are searchable by topic, including "Anti-Israel Activity & BDS."

Foundation for Middle East Peace (FMEP)
1761 N Street NW
Washington, D.C. 20036
(202) 855-3650
email: info@fmep.org
website: www.fmep.org

The Foundation for Middle East Peace is a nonprofit organization dedicated to aiding in the peace process between Israel and Palestine. "The Foundation advances this goal through education, publications about the conflict, a speakers' program to introduce Israeli, Palestinian, and other experts to US audiences, public speaking by officers of the Foundation, and a small grant program to support groups that advance the cause of peace in Israel and Palestine." Every day FMEP produces an Israeli and Palestinian news update. Additionally, they publish a weekly report of Israeli settlement activity in the West Bank and a summary of Israel-related activity in the US Congress. Their website contains a wealth of materials for those interested in Israeli-Palestinian affairs.

The Maccabee Task Force

email: contact@mactaskforce.org
website: https://www.maccabeetaskforce.org

The Maccabee Task Force was created in 2015 by billionaire American philanthropists Sheldon Adelson and Haim Saban to combat the spread of anti-Semitism on America's college campuses. The organization sees the BDS movement as a major force in spreading anti-Semitism on university campuses. They believe that BDS is an anti-Semitic movement that goes beyond legitimate criticism of Israel and attempts to demonize Israel and its supporters. The Maccabee Task Force attempts to help students combat BDS by bringing them the strategies and resources they need to support Israel. Their website offers a newsletter, videos, and other resources designed to defend Israel from BDS activities.

The Middle East Institute

1761 N Street NW
Washington, D.C. 20036
(202) 785-1141
email: information@mei.edu
website: www.mei.com

The Middle East Institute has worked since 1946 to disseminate unbiased information concerning the Middle East to create a more clear understanding of the area's politics, culture, and issues for US policy makers, business leaders, and students. The MEI hosts lectures and conferences featuring Middle East experts who hold diverse views on the region's issues. They offer programs in everything from Middle East arts and culture to countering terrorism. Their website contains myriad materials, including videos, research, and classes. A recent article title was "Gaza fails to capture the world's attention," which examines two completely different perspectives on the Gaza strip, from both the Israeli and Palestinian points of view.

OneVoice

P.O Box 1577-OCS
New York, NY 10113
(212) 897-3985
email: info@OneVoiceMovement.org
website: www.onevoicemovement.org

The OneVoice Movement is a global initiative that supports grassroots activists in Israel, Palestine, and throughout the world who are working to build the human infrastructure needed to create conditions for a just and negotiated settlement to the Israeli-Palestinian conflict. They envision an independent and viable Palestine and a secure Israel free from conflict, where Palestinians and Israelis are able to realize their national and individual goals, and construct a future based upon principles of security, justice, dignity and peace. In addition to its US presence, OneVoice has offices in London, Palestine, and Israel, and information on these offices can be found on its website. Their website also contains information on current events in Israel and Palestine.

Palestinian BDS National Committee

website: https://bdsmovement.net/bnc
email: info@bdsmovement.net
The Palestinian BDS National Committee "is the broadest Palestinian civil society coalition that works to lead and support the BDS movement for Palestinian rights."

Its member organizations include the Council of National and Islamic Forces in Palestine, the General Union of Palestinian Workers, the Palestinian General Federation of Trade Unions, the Palestinian Trade Union Coalition for BDS (PTUC-BDS), the

Palestinian NGO Network (PNGO), and dozens of others. Some of their activities include campaigning with BDS activists locally and worldwide by preparing and disseminating BDS statements and through public speaking, advocating by briefing and lobbying policy makers, conducting media outreach in Palestine and abroad based on a professional media strategy, developing the BDS campaign in other countries, coordinating with BDS activists worldwide, and raising awareness about BDS. Their website includes an explanation of the BDS movement, information on how to get involved, information on various campaigns, and much more.

Permanent Observer Mission of the State of Palestine to the United Nations
115 East 65th Street
New York, NY 10065
(212) 288-8500
email: palestine@un.int
website: http://palestineun.org

The Permanent Observer Mission of the State of Palestine to the United Nations is the formal title of the Palestinian Ambassador to the United Nations. The mission prepares a yearly report on a following every session of the United Nations General Assembly (UNGA). The main purpose for the preparation of this report is to understand voting patterns of U.N. Member States on resolutions related to the Question of Palestine (QoP). The website contains daily briefings on the situation in Palestine, which is especially helpful during times of conflict. For example, during the period surrounding the opening of the US embassy in Jerusalem, daily reports monitored the accompanying Palestinian protests. The website also contains numerous documents, fact sheets, conference news, UN resolutions, and more.

Bibliography of Books

Tom Anderson. *Targeting Israeli Apartheid: A Boycott Divestment and Sanctions Handbook*. London, UK: Corporate Watch, 2011.

Jed L. Babbin and Herbert I. London, *The BDS War against Israel: The Orwellian Campaign to Destroy Israel Through the Boycott, Divestment and Sanctions Movement*. New York, NY: The London Center for Policy Research, 2014.

Omar Barghouti, Naomi Klein, Ra'anan Alexandrowicz, Merav Amir, and Hind Awwad. *The Case for Sanctions against Israel*. London,UK: Verso, 2012.

Umar-S. Barghūtī. *Boycott, Divestment, Sanctions: The Struggle for Palestinian Civil Rights*. Chicago, Il: Haymarket, 2011.

Noam Chomsky and Ilan Pappé. *On Palestine*. London, UK: Penguin Books, 2015

Alan Dershowitz. *The Case Against BDS: Why Singling Out Israel for Boycott Is Anti-Semitic and Anti-Peace*. New York, NY: Bombardier Books, 2018.

Kareem Estefan, Carin Kuoni, and Laura Raicovich. *Assuming Boycott: Resistance, Agency and Cultural Production*. New York, NY: OR Books, 2017

Sunaina Maira, *Boycott!: The Academy and Justice for Palestine*. Oakland, CA: Univ. of California Press, 2018.

Philip Mendes and Nick Dyrenfurth. *Boycotting Israel Is Wrong: The Progressive Path Towards Peace between Palestinians and Israelis*. Sydney, Australia: Univ. of New South Wales Press, 2015.

Cary Nelson and Gabriel Brahm. *The Case against Academic Boycotts of Israel*. Detroit, MI: Wayne State Univ. Press, 2015.

Alpaslan Özerdem, *Conflict Transformation and the Palestinians: The Dynamics of Peace and Justice Under Occupation.* New York, NY: Routledge, Taylor & Francis Group, 2017.

Andrew Pessin and Doron S. Ben-Atar, *Anti-zionism on Campus: The University, Free Speech, and BDS.* Bloomington, IN: Indiana Univ. Press, 2018.

Mazin B. Qumsiyeh, *Popular Resistance in Palestine: A History of Hope and Empowerment.* London,UK: Pluto, 2011.

Barry Shaw, *Fighting Hamas, BDS and Anti-Semitism: Fighting violence, bigotry and hate.* CreateSpace, 2015.

Rich Wiles, *Generation Palestine: Voices from the Boycott, Divestment and Sanctions Movement.* London, UK: Pluto Press, 2013.

Index